BUILDING BONDS

This book contains discussions of mental health that some readers may find triggering including: depression, suicide, self-harm, trauma, abuse, neglect and eating disorders. Turn to page 226 for a list of helpful resources.

A STUDIO PRESS BOOK
First published in the UK in 2025 by Studio Press,
an imprint of Bonnier Books UK,
5th Floor, HYLO, 103-105 Bunhill Row,
London, EC1Y 8LZ
Owned by Bonnier Books,
Sveavägen 56, Stockholm, Sweden
www.bonnierbooks.co.uk

Copyright © by YMHW Consultancy Limited 2025

1 3 5 7 9 10 8 6 4 2

All rights reserved

ISBN 978-1-80078-722-3
E-book ISBN: 978-1-83587-311-3

Edited by Frankie Jones
Designed by Alessandro Susin
Production by Giulia Caparrelli

The views in this book are the author's own and the copyright, trademarks and names are that of their respective owners and are not intended to suggest endorsement, agreement, affiliation or otherwise of any kind.

A CIP catalogue record for this book is available from the British Library
Printed and bound in Great Britain by Clays Lts, Elcograf S.p.A

BUILDING BONDS

Why We Choose the People We Choose *(and how to change it if we want to)*

ZOË ASTON

Introduction	6
Chapter One: **Self**	17
Chapter Two: **Boundaries, Wants and Needs and Attachment Styles**	39
Chapter Three: **Family Relationships**	48
Chapter Four: **Friendships**	84
Chapter Five: **Romantic Relationships**	117
Chapter Six: **Workplace Relationships**	162
Chapter Seven: **Online and Digital Relationships**	187
A Final Note	217
Further Reading and Weblinks	221
Where to find further support	226
Glossary	228
About the author and Reflections	233

INTRODUCTION

As I was sitting in the staff room of a Harley Street treatment centre aged 28, a much older and wiser therapist said to me, 'I think you'd be the perfect person to help others navigate their relationships.' After a moment absorbing the shock of what I'd just heard, I replied 'Me?' and started laughing.

I was really good at tackling addiction issues, was trained in working with childhood trauma and had a reputation for being able to hold excellent boundaries, but actively offering support to other people in their day-to-day relationships seemed like a ridiculous suggestion.

I was perpetually single and put that down to either there being something wrong with me or the way I was enjoying my life. It didn't seem to fit well with the dating world. I'd only had one long term romantic relationship. My immediate family relationships were close. I saw my mum, dad and sister often but tended to feel quite misunderstood by them. This was often a source of pain for me and to this day I still only have very distant connections with my other relatives.

Although I tend to collect friends wherever I go in adulthood, I had no childhood friends and often felt lonely. Most of my work colleagues were much older than me. How could I possibly be a good candidate for helping others with relationships?

Well, it's taken me the best part of a decade to figure out that I am a good candidate for helping others navigate relationships because I know what it feels like to struggle within relationships.

I know what it feels like to be in the depth of self-loathing, what it is like to feel like you have no friends, to be an outsider, to be bullied, dumped, rejected, abandoned, misunderstood and heartbroken. I know what it's like to feel uncared about, to feel left behind. I know the pain of being the only person among my peers who doesn't have a partner, and also how it feels to be rejected from a friendship group. I know the hopelessness that can come with the relationship struggle.

Because of the above, I also know what it feels like to rebuild

INTRODUCTION

my self-worth from scratch and hold on to it even in the face of unhelpful and unhealthy relationships. I know how hard it feels to embrace boundaries with close family members in order to protect my wellbeing. I know the hard work that goes into making friends as an adult and the joy in finding a partner who wants to share his life with me. And most recently, I know what it means to be a parent and love someone in the most terrifying way, that makes my heart feel like it's dancing every single day. It's these knowhows, along with my professional qualifications and 12 years of experience, that qualify me to talk about and guide others through the maze of relationships.

One of the big 'ah-ha' moments for me was learning that my self-worth and my relationships with others are always interacting with each other. And directly impacting the people I was choosing to keep in my life. The more self-worth I had, the less painful my relationships became in the long run, because, as I came to fully understand, how other people behave (or have behaved in the past) isn't a reflection of my self-worth, it's a reflection of theirs.

There are hundreds of books out there pushing the concept that we *need to be doing self-care, that we should work on our self-esteem and that self-love needs to be in place before we can love others*. I disagree. We need people to love us before we can love ourselves. We need someone else to show us our worth before we can internalise it. The self-care, esteem and love that we hear about will fall into place, but they won't be our focus throughout this book, they'll happen as a by-product instead via a deeper understanding and putting practical changes into action. Our focus will be on supporting you to heal the psychological wounds that rob you of your choices in relationships, and to build stronger, healthier and more satisfying connections that contribute to the lifestyle you want and a stronger sense of self-worth.

I have included plenty of practical exercises throughout, some of which have helped me and the people I have supported over the years, and some of which I've developed in hindsight because I feel they really could have helped me or someone else. But our emphasis here will be on better understanding what happens to you and within you in relationships, and empowering how to consciously choose the people to keep in your life.

This leads me to one very important fact, that you must hold in mind throughout this whole book: understanding and defining your relationships, more often than not, means understanding and defining yourself within your relationships. Therefore, we will be starting with your relationship with yourself, and then work through family, friends, romance, workplace relationships and finally online relationships. To break this down further and make myself very clear: we cannot define others through this work, we can only focus on ourselves and our contribution to the ***relational dynamic***.

Your focus needs to be on your input, your thoughts, your feelings, your behaviours, rather than changing or impacting others. You are going to make your own choices. I'll remind you of this as we go, but for now, take a moment to consider your motivation(s) whilst doing the exercise below.

Exercise: Brainstorming

Grab a pen and paper, or use the notes section in the back of this book.

If you're anything like me, you'll read that and absolutely not do it. I get it, maybe you're reading this in bed, on a device or listening to an audio recording. Maybe you're on public transport or your kid is sleeping on you and it's an inconvenient suggestion, or too much effort to do the writing bit.

If you can write stuff down, great. If you are set on doing this in your head, then fine, but know that you won't have a written record of your thoughts and ideas and you might forget them – I always do. This stands for all further exercises in this book.

Write down or imagine the words 'relationship' and 'bonding'. Circle them. Now let yourself free fall about all the things that come to your mind in association with these words.

Here's an example:

In the diagram opposite I can see that my focus is on feeling safe and comfortable in relationships. So, my motivation while I do

INTRODUCTION

this work could be to find safety in my relationships. Your focus might be on something different: you might want to be more intimate, vulnerable, to hold firmer boundaries, to be able to let love in more than you do right now... anything is possible.

From the words you've collected can you see what your focus indicates? Can you spot any motives or themes that interest or surprise you? There is no right or wrong – whatever you uncover is your truth in this moment. So, no judging yourself. Just observe, acknowledge and move on.

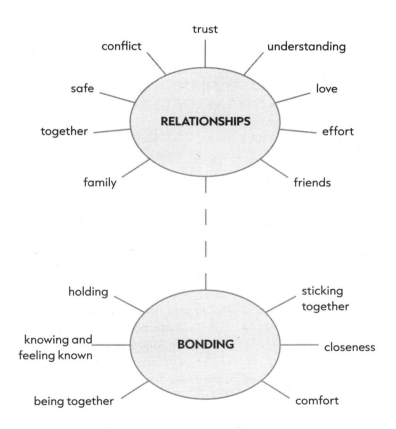

THIS BOOK WILL HELP YOU TO UNDERSTAND

- What your behaviours in relationships might mean.
- How your history impacts how you choose people.
- Why most of other people's behaviour has nothing to do with you and your value.
- How to adjust dysfunctional and unhelpful reactions and behaviours in yourself.
- How to cope with hurtful and damaging experiences like feeling rejected, abandoned and betrayed by others.
- How to relate to others with an idea of what you need and want, in whatever format of relationship you choose.
- How to always feel able to hold on to your self-worth.
- How to change who you choose to be in relationships with.

THE *BUILDING BONDS* DEFINITION OF RELATIONSHIPS AND BONDS (FOR THE SAKE OF CLARITY)

Practical changes are hard to make without an agreed definition of what we are changing. Although a definition of the words 'relationship' and 'bond' may seem like a funny thing to spend your valuable time on, I think it's worth breaking it down to make sure you know what these words mean to you.

Exercise: Reflection

Take a moment now to reflect on what your definition of the word 'relationship' is. You may like to use some of the words you came up with in the previous exercise to get you started.

Oxford Languages defines 'relationship' as:

1. The way in which two or more people or things are connected, or the state of being connected.
2. The state of being connected by blood or marriage.
3. The way in which two or more people or groups regard each other.

Do any of these descriptions help you think about your own definition of relationships?

What if I replace the word 'relationship' with 'bond'?

Oxford Languages defines 'bond' as:

1. A relationship between people or groups based on shared feelings, interests, or experiences.
2. Join or be joined securely to something else.

Based on all I've covered above and my personal and professional experience of building bonds, for the sake of this book, I would define the word 'relationship' as:

A grounded feeling of connection to myself which enables me to bond with people outside of myself.

INSTILLING HOPE

I always put a focus on hope in my work because it has single-handedly pulled me through the darkest moments of my life. My ability to hope has survived everything I've put it through in my personal life and has supported a great many people professionally over the years.

I see instilling hope as a primary requirement as a therapist. If a person doesn't have hope, they tend not to find much reason to invest time and effort towards the possibility of choice or change. That's not to say that if you're a bit hopeless you shouldn't bother, I've worked with clients who need me to hold on to hope for them before they are able to hope for themselves.

I have no idea why, but I understand that I am a naturally hopeful person, and in order to make sure I have covered all my bases I also have to own that it doesn't always work; nothing always works. I've certainly supported people who've eventually lost all hope and sadly felt they couldn't continue in this world. My heart aches when I think of each of them and the amount of pain they must have been in to make that choice. In my comparative clinical experience, it's a rare choice to make and follow through with, and hard to understand fully because those people are not here to help us understand it. What we do know is that a total loss of hope often has its roots in our social lives and its biggest contributing factor seems to be a severely damaged sense of self-worth that leads us to feel we've run out of options. I have included a couple of books in the Further Reading section should you wish to find out more.

In her book *Atlas of the Heart* Brené Brown talks about hope as 'a function of struggle' and here I may find the answer to my query about why I am a hopeful person – because I have struggled. Brown says that we build hopefulness when we are faced with 'discomfort and adversity'. This really speaks to me because hope, as much as it is positioned as a positive experience, is actually constructed out of experiencing emotions such as fear, heartbreak, love, sadness, grief and anger.

It's easy to lose your way when feelings like those listed above bubble up. I invite you to reframe them and think about how hope is constructed within you. If it helps, you can use my voice, as you perceive it throughout this book, to support you continue building your future. What should happen over time is that you both *internalise* my hope and support as well as actively construct your own to support from within.

The trouble with hope

As I've already said, hope doesn't always work out. But sometimes there is a reason for that. Some of us have trouble with the concept of hoping because our internal voices kick off with phrases like 'don't get your hopes up' or 'hope for the best and expect the worst'. When you say negative things to yourself and don't really allow yourself to fully invest in the *felt sense* of hope, you are engaging in a protective strategy that prevents you from feeling the negative emotions listed above that can in fact help construct authentic hope. When we are using a protective stategy we may also feel disappointment and resentment, two feelings that often evolve when instilling hope isn't going the way you'd expected. When you're in this process you are also on a slippery slope towards shaming yourself for not getting something 'right' before you've even tried.

I find shame and disappointment to be two of the most undesirable feelings. I will go out of my way and even lie to myself in order to avoid these emotions. The way to get around this is to separate hope from expectation. Unmet expectations are what lead us into disappointment and, ultimately, resentment because unmet expectations are conditional on outcomes; put differently, we make a choice based on what we think the outcome will be rather than because it's the best thing for our wellbeing.

Hope, however, is not attached to the outcome. It doesn't form attachments to what happens next. It's a far less judgmental way of thinking about things. If something doesn't go the way you hoped, hope can allow you to bounce back and move you forward once again, without expectation or judgement about what just happened.

Exercise: Nurturing a hope habit:

We all hope in slightly different ways and instilling hope is about you figuring out what type of hope to hold on to when things feel easy – and also when they feel hard. Here are four types of hope. See which one feels most familiar to you:

Realistic hope: *Orientated towards incremental changes. For example: 'I hope, after a good night's sleep, I feel a little bit better in the morning.'*

Utopian hope: *Contemplates what's happening right now and brings hope and power together to hold out hope for the future. Protests and movement groups like Black Lives Matter, Extinction Rebellion and Me Too are a great example of utopian hope.*

Chosen hope: *The hopeful feeling you choose to have even when things are happening to you or around you that leave you feeling helpless and powerless. For example: 'Things feel awful right now and I really hope something will happen to bring about change in the near future.'*

> ***Transcendent hope:*** *When hope is part of your daily being and personality. It's a general feeling of optimism and hopefulness about the future. For example, living by the following mantras: 'This too shall pass' and 'One day at a time'.*
>
> *If you do not identify with any of these definitions of hope, ask yourself the following:*
>
> - *Is there anyone in your life who you view as hopeful?*
> - *What do you like about the way they express hope about things?*
> - *Can you imagine yourself borrowing a bit of their hope for a while?*
>
> *If life feels hopeless a lot of the time, it is a good idea to speak to a therapist or mental health professional. You will find ways of contacting mental health professionals on pages 225-226.*

HOW TO USE THIS BOOK

This book is split into six chapters. Chapter One ('Self') looks at your relationship with yourself, Chapter Two is a short chapter which provides essential information about boundaries, wants and needs and attachment styles, Chapter Three focuses on Family Relationships, Chapter Four covers Friendships, Chapter Five looks at Romantic Relationships and dating, Chapter Six is all about Workplace Relationships and Chapter Seven explores Online and Digital Relationships.

Each main chapter starts with a reflective statement for you to ponder, before providing an in-depth exploration of each type of relationship and several practical exercises. I've structured the information offered to reflect the developmental process of each relationship and the different choices that can be made along the way, and why.

For example: how it begins, what the journey of that relationship generally looks like throughout your lifespan, and the effect that your choices can have on you, both positive and negative. We will also focus on how to work with difficulties and differences which will include resolving conflict and how to communicate more effectively, as well as support to help you move on from relationships that no longer serve you, should you choose to.

The chapters and indeed the subtitled sections, stand alone in their own right so you can read them in any order and refer to them at any time. I do urge you to read the information in the order I have written it as the book builds on itself. However, if you do choose to read things out of order, I have cross-referenced as much as possible so you can read the connecting information.

We are going to cover a lot of ground and it's likely that not everything will apply to you right now... At the very end of each chapter is a summary which includes the main messages we've covered. Reading this will help you condense the information so you can come back to it when you feel it is more relevant to you and your life.

It's to be expected, when you are reading about relationships, that you start to think of the people in your life who 'should' know, read, understand or reflect on the same messages. In my experience, it is *impossible* to get someone to read a book if they don't want to. BUT you might just be able to get them to take 60 seconds to read the summary and then, maybe you can share what you learned with them verbally. If they will not even read the summary in their own time, read it to them and see if it sparks any interest. If that's not realistic, do yourself a favour and let it go – focus on yourself.

At the back of the book, you'll find further reading lists and web links for each chapter, as well as guidance on contacting mental health professionals and support teams. On pages 228-232 you will also find a glossary of terms. If I have not defined a term within the main text of the book, the first use of each defined term will appear as ***bold italic*** text and be defined in the glossary. If you don't know what something means, please read the definition as it'll support your understanding of the content.

Before we get started I need you to know that...
In relationships, and pretty much all of life, there are two types

of learning: the theoretical learning that you hold in your mind, and the empirical learning that turns theory into practice. It is too easy to read a book, absorb some of the information and then do nothing with it. We all do it. I'm guilty too.

The problem with this is that having the information and doing nothing with it tends to cause us more emotional torment and cognitive dissonance (see p. 122-123) as our choices no longer match what we know.

As you start to unveil the truth about the things that have happened in your life and the choices you've made as a result, you may feel sad, angry, hopeless and even depressed for a short time. Use these feelings to help construct hope and to motivate you rather than discourage you.

Feeling better comes when you are empowered to change, and change only happens once you fully understand, on an emotional and intellectual level, what choices you need to make to maintain it.

You are in charge of this process; you dictate the pace and you get to make the decisions about how it goes. I will give you the information and guidance on how to implement it, but you need to be the one to apply it.

Summary

1. *You're reading this book to let go of unhelpful patterns and build strong and healthy relationships with yourself and others.*
2. *Our working definition of relationship for the sake of this book is 'A grounded feeling of connection to myself which enables me to bond with people outside of myself'.*
3. *Expectations can lead to shame and disappointment. We will work on letting them go.*
4. *While hope is an important part of this journey, you just need a little bit of it to make things work.*

Chapter One:
SELF

Reflective question: How are the choices you make in relation to others defined by your relationship with yourself? How are the choices you make in relation to yourself defined by your relationship with others?

The work we are doing involves thinking about countless people that have entered and exited your life, but after all is said and done, you are left with you, so we'll start by exploring your relationship with yourself. The thing is, your relationship with yourself evolves out of your relationship with others, and the choices you make in relation to others are defined by your relationship with yourself.

Most of us have had moments in life when we struggled to like, love and care for ourselves. Most of us have also had moments when we wondered why we feel we can't find love and acceptance outside of ourselves. We sometimes hear advice to the effect of 'you'll never be happy until you love yourself' or 'you need to like yourself before you'll be able to accept love from anyone else'. Messaging like this, to my mind, can not only be unhelpful, it's also untrue, simply because we learn to love by being shown love. And you cannot do that on your own.

Although I disagree with the idea that you need to find self-love before you find love in others, I do subscribe to the idea that, as an adult, you need to be content with your self-worth and how you relate to yourself.

Some of the messages we receive about the self-relationship are based in psychology theory (which we'll cover) but some can have an undesirable impact on us. Messages like 'who you are is an amalgamation of the five people you spend the most time with' and 'look at the company you keep, it reflects who you are' can have a negative impact on our mental health, particularly if our self-worth is already struggling, as we will latch on to anything that might explain away the unwelcome feelings we have about ourselves. My main issue with these messages is that they can encourage people to edit the other people in their lives rather than encourage them to look at themselves.

Some of these ideas may stem from experiments in the 1970s that helped establish Social Identity Theory (SIT, founded by Henry Tajfel) and go even further back to psychology founders like Freud. SIT is about the dynamics of belonging. It looks at how we understand and interpret our own social behaviour in relation to others and the consequences of considering ourselves as part of a group... or not. It's true that influence from others is an important part of how we relate to ourselves, but if you look into other established psychology theories from pioneers such as Carl Rogers, you'll find a more nuanced approach to understanding 'The Self'. Rogers, as an example, talked about an ideal self and worked to help his clients realise *congruence* between how they are and how they want to be (see Further Reading).

One truth that amalgamates the two ideas above is that when we lack a solid and congruent understanding of our self, we can merge our personalities into those of the people we spend the most time with, by pushing aside our needs, wants, desires and preferences in favour of someone else's. Sometimes that's a helpful thing but at other times it's not and we can become *enmeshed* and abandon ourselves for others. This focus on others rather than self can lead to challenges in coping with rejection, whether it's from a romantic relationship, a social group, job or audition, or a betrayal at work.

Put simply, without a strong sense of self, your concept of who you are, your identity, will feel difficult to maintain. Your identity is what forms the majority of your relationships with yourself, but it also has to come from somewhere – most undoubtedly another relationship. Let's start at the very beginning...

THE VERY BEGINNING (A VERY BRIEF OVERVIEW)

If we look carefully at the map of your relationship with yourself, in reality, it starts with(in) someone else. So, you have always been in a relationship, and you have always had relationship needs. You have always been primed to need bonding, connection and what we call *co-regulation*. You were first in a relationship with your birth parent and then your primary caregiver, who may or may not have been your birth parent. Regardless, we all began life via a bonding experience, and we all needed to know other people before we could even know that we exist ourselves.

As far as an infant is concerned, they have no awareness that they are a separate person from their birthing parent or primary caregiver for at least the first six or seven months outside the womb. They are wholeheartedly merged with their carer and their psychological need is for their carer to regulate them (and ensure their physical survival too). This is an entirely appropriate process of feeling part of another person, that occurs before co-regulation is even possible.

Whether or not we were cared for by a biological parent, how our caregiver responded to our wants and needs in the first three years of our life taught us about the psychological support available to us in the world and set the groundwork for the choices we make in the relationship with our self. This includes how we support and regulate ourselves and how we have learned to relate to others.

As we mature into our identity and our personality starts to develop, if encouraged to follow our natural interests, attitudes and values, we will have started to use our carer for co-regulation which evolves into *self-regulation* by the time we are in our twenties (yes, it's that late!). However, if in order to secure psychological support we are required to conform to a caregiver's expectations of who we should be, or not given the opportunity to move from dependency to interdependency because someone in a position of authority tends to rescue, fix or interfere in our life, we may find our self enmeshed with that person beyond what is considered healthy, unable to understand that we have worth as an individual. Consequently, this sense of disempowerment could lead us to rely on others to dictate our worth as we mature.

PSYCHOLOGICAL SUPPORT

In terms of our relationship with ourselves, I've chosen to focus on four forms of psychological support: self-regulation, mirroring, instilling inherent worth, and our internal working model. I explain them here in turn, and refer to them throughout the rest of the book.

Self-regulation
The term refers to how you monitor and control your behaviour in response to your emotions. It involves witnessing and interacting with your emotions, and knowing what to do about them when they happen. We cannot actively even begin to do this for ourselves until we are about seven years old. Up until then we need a trusted adult (or at the very least someone who is already capable of self-regulating) to psychologically support us in understanding our emotions and regulating them.

A psychologist called Roy Baumeister had a big impact on how the psychology world theorises self-regulation (see Further Reading). He broke the concept down into clear sections: desirable behaviour; motivation to meet standards; monitoring of situations; thoughts that precede breaking standards; and willpower (in other words, how you control your cravings, urges and emotional reactions in life). He also proposed that willpower is a limited resource based on the amount of glucose available to your brain and that a more effective and successful alternative is to choose to create helpful habits instead.

Over the years, studies that tested this theory have also found that self-regulation is limited, depending on what support we've had from others (see Further Reading). This knowledge has a big impact on changes in parenting advice which people are offered, as well as the approach practitioners like myself use to promote healing any emotional damage experienced in childhood. In any of Baumeister's identified sections, there is only a certain amount of possible self-regulation before you need to seek support, which is where co-regulation comes in. If we don't get the co-regulation needed, it can affect the way we function in relationships as well as the foundations for our self-worth.

So, we can learn helpful habits around self-regulation through the psychological support received when co-regulating with another person. We can then step out into the world feeling supported and knowing a bit more about ourselves, aware of how to function and take good care of our needs. When our internal resources run short, and we need other people to support us, we come back to co-regulation. To put it another way, part of having a secure relationship with yourself is knowing that there will *always* be times when we need other people to support our emotional wellbeing because we are unable to do it ourselves.

Mirroring

We mirror one another all the time. It's not a conscious process. In infancy and childhood, mirroring supports our relationship with ourselves as we start to reflect or copy the behaviours that we witness in others.

As we get older and start to experiment with self-regulation and co-regulation, the term 'mirroring' changes slightly, referring more closely to the process of seeing parts of ourselves in others, and vice versa. So as children we learn through watching others and mirroring what we see, while as adults, we use mirroring to move us towards co-regulation, aware of what we've already learned through the same process of reflection. This is why, when we have children, we are often triggered by what our child mirrors back to us about ourselves.

Studies have proven that we mimic (or mirror) each other's posture and physical gestures without realising it – this is called the 'chameleon effect' (see Further Reading). And it's also proven that we can only notice things we recognise. This means that through the mirroring process, if we are observant enough, everyone we come across in life can teach us about ourselves. And more pertinent, within our current discussion, is that through mirroring we also learn about emotional regulation and resilience.

Exercise: Observation

Over the next 24–48 hours, make a note of what you notice in other people. Take some time to reflect on whether what you are noticing about them mirrors something in you. You can also investigate it the other way around – notice something in yourself and reflect on who may be mirroring the aspect of yourself back to you, historically or in the here and now. You may have to dig quite deep, especially if the things you notice are things you don't particularly like (hint: this happens a lot).

Inherent Worth

When I had my daughter, people asked me if she was a 'good baby'. I felt a bit jarred by the question. My therapist head told me that 'no one is born into this world as inherently good or bad. We are all born equal.' So what was I to say in response?

I've learned that when we strip back our circumstances and our material possessions and look at the worth of every baby born, each human has as much worth and is neither better nor worse than the next. If I were to label my daughter as good or bad, surely that would say more about me as a parent than her as a baby. Possibly, it would even mirror back to me more about how I felt about myself as a parent than anything else. Being asked this question so candidly really highlighted how, right from the start of our lives, society tries to define who we are, as good or bad based on what we do, how we look and how we behave, rather than accepting newly formed humans just as they are.

In order to instil my daughter with her own self-worth, my job is to adjust to her, and meet her where she's at, so that she learns to trust that she will be supported physically and psychologically and that all her needs will be met. Believing in inherent worth means passing on the message that we are all loveable, and deserve to have our needs met, even when our behaviours and emotions don't match what others want. Labelling those more vulnerable than us as 'bad' or 'difficult' condemns people to a lifetime of self-worth difficulties because we instil the message that there is something wrong with the identity of the person therefore the message they get is that they need to be different in order to be loved... more on this in the next section.

Your Internal Working Model
My fourth and final category of psychological support systems brings together all the previous categories under the umbrella term of the Internal Working Model of attachment (IWM). This idea was founded by attachment pioneer John Bowlby. Put very simply, our IWM is observing how others treat us and internalising that as information about how to treat ourselves. Put differently, our relationship with ourselves is supported through the care we receive from others.

Our IWM is the sum total of the psychological support we receive, including all of the above, from our primary caregivers. It is ultimately an automatic and unconscious process, and generally remains that way unless it starts to cause problems. A problematic IWM could show up as a lack of desire for self-care: not keeping boundaries with others, self-sabotaging behaviours, a difficulty in accepting care, developing an addiction, an eating disorder or co-dependence. Our IWM is a predictor of our future relationship with ourselves, as well as with others. It creates expectations of how we treat ourselves and expectations of how we'll let others treat us.

For example, a child who experiences a parent or authority figure to be physically or emotionally unavailable, may internalise this to mean that they are not worth being available for. They may then find themselves attracted to unavailable people and become unavailable to care for themselves. They become unavailable to themselves through using external ways of distracting themselves from their difficult emotions as well as their wants and needs, which they haven't yet learned to regulate – because there wasn't enough co-regulation or psychological support around due to a parent or care-giver being unable or unavailable to provide it. And because they have an IWM lacking in self-worth because inherent worth hasn't been instilled, they will find it difficult to receive attention and care from others, and will tend to neglect themselves. Consequently, they will have unstable self-esteem and struggle to hold on to self-worth.

THE DIFFERENCE BETWEEN SELF-ESTEEM AND SELF-WORTH

There are lots of self-help books and other media around about self-esteem, self-love and self-care that encourage us to work on self-worth in order to improve our wellbeing. Some of the advice comes from psychology professionals – but some of it does not, and it can be hard to differentiate between the two.

Self-esteem is how we think and feel about ourselves. It is affected by things that happen in our lives and it's normal for it to change many times through the day. Self-worth, however, is more closely connected to the inherent worth that has been instilled in us and is about how we fundamentally value ourselves. Our self-esteem can change a little and be knocked about a bit without fundamentally undermining our self-worth. But if our self-worth changes it's highly likely that our self-esteem is also affected.

I've found that the concepts that have become rather trendy over the past few years – such as affirmations, gratitude lists, meditation and journalling – seem to be attached to the expectation that we will improve our self-esteem if we do them for a period of time, without an explanation of how they really work and what should shift within our self-worth when we practise them. I often meet people who are aiming for changes in their self-esteem and feeling frustrated that the above concepts haven't had the desired effect, when actually, they really need to create a more sustainable relationship to themselves by focusing on their self-worth rather than self-esteem.

A struggle comes up here if our role models didn't have their own sense of inherent worth and couldn't give us a helpful stencil to follow by affirming us, expressing gratitude and being mindful in relation to us. Our IWM may actively work against exercises like affirmations, meditations and gratitude lists. I cover this and the exercises mentioned above in much more depth in my first book *Your Mental Health Workout* (see Further Reading list).

Chapter One: SELF

> *Exercise: Uncovering Your Internal Working Model*
>
> Cast your mind back through your timeline. Go right back to childhood and even infancy if you can. In your mind, as you run through your life experience, think about your major caregivers (can be parents, childcare professionals, teachers, friends, relatives). Who have you had significant relationships with? And how did they treat you? What did they instil in you about how to treat yourself? How do you feel when you think about this?

WHAT IS OUR PART IN ALL THIS?

Contradiction incoming… Despite the fact that our relationship with ourselves is largely built on what we learn from others, the thing that mobilises us to make different choices in our relationship with ourselves is to stop looking outwards or casting responsibility onto others. (*Ouch!* I know, I feel it too.)

Lots of us are invested in blaming others when life doesn't go quite right, and it's easy to do, but let me ask you outright, do you think blaming others is helpful to your relationship with yourself? Sometimes it might feel like it is because we advocate responsibility of our uninvited feelings. But in reality, we can't control others or change what has happened even when we blame them, even if something is objectively their fault. Blame isn't helpful to our relationship with anyone; in fact, when blame doesn't have the impact we seek, many of us end up turning it inwards on ourselves and blame turned inwards becomes shame. What is helpful, when focusing on ourselves, is to ask the question:

What is my part in this?

When we start to focus on our part, it can feel quite lonely. We all have patterns we play out over and over, metaphorical games and dances as such. Once we start to notice our patterns, we come to realise that much of our behaviour is pre-choreographed by life experiences and what we gained (or didn't gain) from the psychological support received in the first few years of life. From there, we have a choice.

Letting go of blaming others, and of therefore shaming ourselves, means becoming more familiar with our patterns. We can choose to change or give up the games we play, and discard the dances we do in relationships, including the one we have with ourselves, that no longer serve us. Put very simply, we have to let go of the expectation that others are responsible for how we feel, and choose to be accountable for how we feel about being ourselves.

LONELINESS

Loneliness is the void that is created through lack of meaningful social interaction, belonging and connection, but it can also emerge through losing connection with ourselves and when we start a process of letting go of patterns and belief systems that we thought were keeping us safe. It rears its head when we perceive our aloneness to be painful. And loneliness is painful. In fact, loneliness can be so painful that researchers have found it can negatively impact the longevity of our lives by 45 per cent. That percentage is higher than both obesity (20 per cent) and excessive alcohol consumption (30 per cent) (see Further Reading).

When we are feeling the pain of loneliness, due to a lack of human connection, connection with ourselves or through changes we are choosing to make, we become even more sensitive (sometimes labelled *rejection sensitivity*) to anything or anyone that might reject or abandon us further, and the more pain we are in the riskier it feels to attempt bids for connection. So we isolate ourselves and quit letting others get close to us (see diagram). And, while we sit in our loneliness, our IWM gets going, often with negative self-talk about why we are where we are.

For me, I had to start asking myself, 'What is my part in this?' and 'How can I change it?' My main take away was that I wasn't lacking people in my life, I was attempting to change and through change was struggling to connect with the version of myself that was emerging and therefore finding it hard to connect with others.

Chapter One: SELF

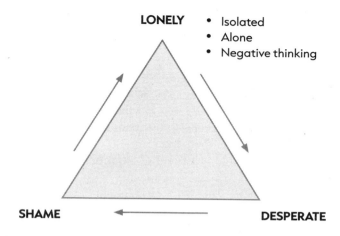

LONELY
- Isolated
- Alone
- Negative thinking

SHAME
- Attempts to understand why by making it about self
- Isolates self further due to shame

DESPERATE
- Hypersensitive to rejection and abandonment
- Flooded with yearning that stems from childhood

Getting honest

A big part of my struggle with myself and subsequent experience of loneliness was down to me not being honest. Whether we are outright lying about things or displaying a more subtle inauthenticity – like not mentioning that we have a different view on a topic, or even saying what we think people want to hear rather than what's true for us – we abandon and sacrifice our connection with ourselves, and this is also what is mirrored back to us when others seem reluctant to connect with us. See the chart overleaf for types of overt and covert dishonesty.

When I realised this is what I had been doing, I decided to be brutally honest with myself in order to get a better sense of what I now refer to as my reality. I started journalling and stopped omitting things in my writing. There were some things that were really hard to write down, but I had to start somewhere. I wrote about how angry I was with loved ones and how guilty I felt about that. I wrote about how much shame I felt towards the way I looked, all the things I felt ungrateful for, my difficulties with maintaining my eating disorder recovery, and how often I still felt like self-harming many years after treatment. Then I started to be more honest with myself verbally, and consequently in my therapy sessions, where I knew I was in a confidential space, I learned to tolerate the feelings of shame, which meant I could be more open while another person witnessed my experience without judgement. I felt my shame start to slip away and I began to feel more connected and less lonely, first in relation to my therapist, and eventually in relation to myself and others too.

The therapy example is a good illustration of the interplay between self-relationship and relationship with others. Therapy is where I started telling the truth to someone I felt safe with. The truth about how I was feeling. I began to tell others the truth more often by saying things like: 'In this moment I'm good. I'm happy to be here and pleased to see you. In general, however, I've been finding things really difficult and I am struggling a lot.' You can see in that dialogue, I didn't need to say exactly what was going on, I just needed to be more honest in a general sense and see what that felt like. I'm not advocating for you to be telling everyone your private pain and asking everyone you meet to know your connection needs. I'm simply advocating for more authenticity and vulnerability in appropriate situations. As you find safe places to do so you'll start to create safety inside yourself and your other relationships, via authenticity and vulnerable expression.

Overt dishonesty:	Covert dishonesty:
Lying	Omission
Cheating	Blaming
Stealing	Shaming
Copying	Silence
Bribing	Comparing
Sabotaging	Dissociating

We do not know how others will respond to us being honest about our reality and as you start to become more authentic, you may find that people either over-focus on what you tell them or ignore it entirely. This unpredictability can bring up anxiety and fear about being more honest, if we are not grounded from within. You may need to be straightforward and direct about what you need from them. For example: tell them you need them to empathise with the feelings you are having, not to try to fix the situation or to tell you everything will be okay. The person you are talking to may or may not be able to meet this need, depending on their emotional intelligence and current state, but the point is to hear yourself say it. You can help yourself out a bit by asking someone who you think will be able to respond by meeting the need, rather than someone who might not. Sometimes all we need to hear is something simple like, 'It sounds like you've has a really difficult week – are you okay?' Expressing emotional needs like this is a vulnerable but very effective way to generate intimacy on all levels. And I think you'll find that telling the truth makes you feel less lonely and less isolated and over time, far more emotionally resilient.

A note on difficult emotions
We tend to think we need to fix the difficult feelings to make them go away, believing that difficult feelings are bad, and we need to get the good ones back. Our relationship with ourselves is about learning to tolerate a full range of emotions, which means being willing to become vulnerable. Even if we've lived a life where other people have been unable to tolerate our vulnerability, as adults we must grant ourselves the opportunity. This is where we see psychological resilience take shape, and self-worth becomes easier to hold on to.

Exercise: Getting honest about your reality

Describe a vulnerability you recognise in yourself and how you are dishonest about it. See the overt/covert dishonesty chart for prompts.

For example: 'I feel rejected very easily' or 'I find it hard to stand up for myself in romantic relationships'. In both these scenarios the dishonesty is in you not stating your needs or holding your boundaries.

How do you feel about this?
For example: do you feel annoyed at yourself for being sensitive to rejection, or do you judge yourself for not being able to stand up for yourself and hold boundaries in place?

Name three specific events where you felt this vulnerability in action.

For example: 'I felt rejected when my friend didn't notice I was(n't) at the party last week' or 'When I was with my girlfriend, I couldn't say that I was angry about how she spoke to me'.

How would you like it to be different next time? And what's your part in it?

For example: 'The next time I feel rejected, I would like to ask for clarification from the other person'. Or: 'The next time I feel angry, I would like to find a healthy way of expressing it'.

What help could you seek to support the above changes?

For example: 'I could ask someone else for help when I feel rejected' or 'I could ask others how they express their anger appropriately and see if there is a way that would suit me to practise'.

Reminder: *this is not about getting rid of your feelings or your vulnerability; this is about learning to manage your emotions in healthy ways and feeling authentically connected to your reality, being more honest with yourself and developing a strong and resilient self relationship that'll improve your quality of life.*

CHANGING HOW YOU FEEL ABOUT YOURSELF

Building Self-Esteem

My definition of self-esteem remains the same as when I wrote *Your Mental Health Workout*. Self-esteem means: *we feel aligned, balanced, equal and worthy.* And for this particular book I would like to add: *in relation to ourselves and others*. As explained previously, self-worth is a slightly different thing – it is less easily affected by our circumstances and environment, therefore harder to build yet easier to maintain.

You can build self-esteem, quite simply by engaging in esteemable actions – actions that give you the message that you are good enough. Things like eating well, exercising, attending to your social life, and turning up on time for your commitments are all esteemable acts. Helping others is another really good esteemable act. Some people need to start with the actions and the internal message will follow, while others need to do it the other way around: change the messages you give yourself and the actions will become possible. The messages or self-talk you want to be engaging in are things like: I am equal, My feelings are important, I am worthy, I matter, I am good enough.

> **Exercise: *Understanding fluctuations in your Self-Esteem***
>
> *Next time you are in a group of people, maybe on public transport, in your office, or at a party, take a moment to observe your thinking. Are you comparing yourself to others? Are you thinking something along the lines of 'She's prettier than I am', or 'They obviously don't know what they are doing', or 'He is so much smarter than me'? If you listen carefully to yourself, you might find thoughts like these and many more swimming around in your mind.*
>
> *Each of these thoughts moves you out of your self-esteem either into better than or less than. Noticing your thinking is the first step to monitoring your relationship with yourself more closely, and therefore getting to know yourself better.*
>
> ***Take it further:***
> *Once you've noticed the thoughts, see if you can actively withdraw your judgement and come back to being equal. Repeating the mantra 'I am equal' will help you.*

One of the psychological support systems we covered earlier was the idea of inherent worth. Knowing you have inherent worth means you know you are equal. Equal to everyone else. You are not better than or less than. You are just as good or as bad as others. I'll say it again – human beings are not worth more than each other. In fact, it's our tendency to rank ourselves against others that contributes to chronic self-worth difficulties and problematic power exchanges, and can lead to things like sexism, racism, ableism and *childism*. Any time you are feeling better than or worse than others, your self-esteem is having a wobble and your relationship with yourself is taking the hit.

Most of us are exceedingly familiar with feeling less than, when we feel a bit rubbish about ourselves, and we are aware that we are on the receiving end of someone else believing they are 'better than' us, which can include any kind of 'ism'. We don't always realise that feeling better than others is an equally unhealthy place to be. In addition, if you are shuddering at the idea that you are equal to others, it's probably because you've confused healthy self-esteem with arrogance. Furthermore, at some point in your life, you may have been shamed or witnessed someone being shamed for being arrogant, or been in a relationship with someone who displayed traits of *narcissism*.

Stabilising Self-Worth
For me, the journey towards a solid sense of self-worth and changing how I felt about myself was much deeper than the work I did on my self-esteem. It included a commitment to a *re-parenting* therapy model that supported me to meet all of my inner children (or parts of myself), change how I was caring for them and develop those internal relationships. Through this I began to value and see worth in the parts of me that I did like as well as the parts that I didn't. It worked because I found belonging and connection within myself.

Choosing this approach for my relationship with myself has been one of the most empowering and life-changing choices I've made, and is most likely the move that helped me hold on to my self-worth as an adult, through difficulties with friends, family, romance, work relationships and navigating the world of online relationships too. Committing to this work meant becoming mindful about which parts of me were being stimulated in different scenarios and why. Rather than reacting with my pre-choreographed patterns and getting upset, feeling angry, blaming others, shaming myself or isolating and withdrawing from the world, I started to look inwards, to meet the needs of the inner parts of myself. Through the re-parenting approach I changed my IWM.

What seems to come up a lot when I do this work with clients (and I experienced it too) is that it's all very well accessing your inner ten-year-old and identifying how they feel, but what then? As we have learned already, we need to be taught how to take care of ourselves, and if self-worth hasn't been instilled the re-parenting part of this process is a really hard thing to do.

Here's a personal example: My lack of self-worth seemed to make me a target for teasing throughout school, but when I was 13 I was being bullied because of a rumour that was spread about me. Later in life, as a 25-year-old, I would find myself going out of my way to avoid walking past groups of schoolchildren. A part of me was still terrified of them. Suddenly, in such moments, I was no longer my 25-year-old self with a Master's degree in psychology. Noticing a group of teenagers had the power to plummet me back into that familiar 13-year-old space where I felt ashamed of myself, unequal, constantly under attack and, most noticeably, very unworthy and unsafe.

What I now realise is that when I was being bullied, the kids frightened me, but worse were the adults around me who did not look after me. Teachers would tell me that it would pass. There was a sense that it 'wasn't that bad' and that I was being 'oversensitive', or worse, that I had done something to cause the bullying. I lost any sense of self-worth because the authority figures I sought for help didn't support me to make my school life safe. That is where the real damage was done. The message I received from the authority figures was that I wasn't to be believed; my truth and my reality weren't worth acting on and were minimised and ignored. So this is what I internalised and how I treated myself going forward.

When we are not shown the best way to look after ourselves and we don't feel there are people in our life who unconditionally support us, there will be a gap where our self-worth should have been instilled. Imagine how my experience could have been different if the adults around me had taken my words seriously and taken the time to understand how awful being around other teenagers had become. Most likely I would have felt understood, connected with and respected. As a result, I may have been able to attribute those qualities to how I treated myself internally and come out of that experience with a better sense of how to look after myself in any similar situations.

My self-worth started to repair when I became willing to have an internal dialogue that rebuilt trust with my 13-year-old self. I dialogued with her about the bullying, and more importantly had the conversations with her that should have been had in real time. I needed a therapist to role model these conversations for me so I could start to separate myself from the traumatic experience and not be taken down by the feeling of shame anymore.

The 13-year-old Zoë needed to hear that she didn't deserve what she was getting, that there was nothing wrong with her and she shouldn't have been left in such an awfully vulnerable position; it should never have happened. Once I had learned from my therapist how to do this self-worth work – the dialogue with my younger self, boundaries started to feel possible, so should anyone reactivate or challenge my experience in any way, the internal boundaries I developed through my healing kept me safe.

I hope sharing a snapshot of my personal experience and how I learned to dialogue with myself is relatable and helps you decide which parts of you need attending to, in order to create a sense of self-worth that sticks. To further this, below are a couple of observation exercises that I often give clients and readers to try out. I've followed them up with a visualisation exercise to help you build a dialogue with the wounded parts of you.

Exercise: Observation

Look in the mirror each morning and evening for one week, and simply observe what you see. Notice where your attention falls and what happens in your thinking and your emotions. You may notice some uncomfortable feelings around the things you see that you do not like about yourself. Work with this. Stay with it. Try not to pass judgement (and notice if you do). You may also, in time, not only observe your physical body but find that this exercise also connects you with what's happening in your relationship towards different parts of yourself too.

Take it further:
Fill in the gaps in the sentences below and repeat, either in your head or out loud, three times:

'I notice I feel _____ about my _____ and I accept myself anyway.'

You could write your completed sentence in the notes section of this book. Or on your phone, or on a piece of scrap paper – whatever suits you best.

This is a really gentle way to naturally get to know how you are relating to yourself currently, and is worth coming back to intermittently in life to see how things are changing.

Here's another abbreviated version of an exercise I give people when they are starting to work on relating to themselves differently.

Reflective Exercise

Step 1: Ask yourself: 'What can I do today that allows me to be responsible and accepting towards myself and gives me the message that I am good enough?'

When you answer this question, remember your relationship with yourself includes all the different parts of self, the 13-year-old, the 3-year-old, the angry part, the sad part, the happy part, and so on.

Actions such as having commitments, helping others, advocating for yourself, standing up for what you believe in and doing it (in other words, boundaries), regardless of what the chatter in your mind is telling you about yourself, can help improve your relationship with yourself.

> *Take it Further*
> On a day when you sense your self-worth is in a good place, visualise your younger self at a time when you were going through something difficult, something which had an impact on how you feel about yourself. How old are you? What are you wearing? Where are you? What is the expression on your face? What are the conversations that you needed to have? What does the child in you need to hear?
> If you have a sense of what needs to be said, go ahead and start the dialogue. If you feel a bit lost with that second part, just hold on to the image of the child, and as you continue to work on yourself, the dialogue will come in time.

SAYING YES (AND NO) TO CHANGE

Humans prefer familiarity over change. Even if familiar is uncomfortable, we often choose it. When someone changes, even if the change is in their best interest, it can upset the equilibrium for the person who is changing and also those who are in relationship to them. As an example, before you decided to work on your relationships, you may have said 'yes' to everything and rarely expressed an opinion. As you build or re-build your self-esteem and self-worth, you'll have a more rounded idea of what you want and need, and as a result you know how to say 'yes' and how to say 'no'. People who've relied on you not being able to say no or not having an opinion will find this difficult.

As you work on your relationship with yourself you might notice you are creating and maintaining different boundaries with people and find you are responding in a more grounded manner instead of getting caught up in unhelpful relationship dynamics. These types of changes are courageous and brave and at times may be observed by others as a negative thing either because they don't know how to adjust to your changes, or have not been expecting it.

The vulnerability exercise we did earlier in this chapter, as well as practising being honest with yourself, will provide you

Chapter One: SELF

with the foundations you need for being able to represent yourself with both esteem and worth.

Below is one last exercise for your relationship with yourself before we move on to the rest of the work, which will all be about your relationship with others.

Exercise: How to say yes and how to say no – and mean it!

An important part of representing yourself and dealing with conflict is knowing how to say yes and no. It sounds simple, so firstly may I ask you to reflect on how many times you've said yes to something and then wondered why you agreed to it. Or maybe you're more likely to say no and then feel like you missed out and regretted it?

If you can't say yes or no to things honestly, you will struggle to set limits in life and represent who you are. Your relationship with yourself will suffer more than any other relationship. Being able to say yes and no, and to mean it, is a really important part of assuring you get the co-regulation you need and that you get your personal needs met. Difficulties with honestly saying yes and no usually results in you feeling overextended, victimised, used, anxious and unhappy.

If you cannot say no, you'll never know when your 'yes' is authentic. So that is where we will start.

Part One: Complete the following sentences:

1. When I say no, I think _____
2. When I say no, I feel _____
3. When I say no, I act _____

Reflect on your answers and note down which beliefs are interacting or interfering with your ability to say no.

Some of us have no problem in saying no to things, whereas saying yes can cause tension and anxiety. So, let's look at what happens when you say yes to things.

BUILDING BONDS

Part Two: Complete the following sentences:

1. *When I say yes, I think* _____
2. *When I say yes, I feel* _____
3. *When I say yes, I act* _____

Take it Further:
Reflect on your answers and note down which beliefs are interacting or interfering with your ability to say yes.

We have reached the end of Chapter One. We have started to build your awareness of who you are and laid the groundwork for consistent and sustainable change in all your relationships. You've learned how and why your relationship with yourself has a fair amount to do with other people, and the work you've done so far will help work on the relationships you have with others. You'll find that the work on your relationship with yourself continues to evolve through the other chapters in this book.

The reflective question at the start of this section was: How are the choices you make in relation to others defined by your relationship with yourself? How are the choices you make in relation to yourself defined by your relationship with others?

What do you think now, having finished the chapter?

Summary

1. *Your relationship with yourself grows out of your relationship with others.*
2. *Self-worth is instilled very early in life.*
3. *Self-esteem is different to self-worth.*
4. *Your Internal Working Model (IWM) informs how you treat yourself.*
5. *Being honest with yourself is the best thing you can do to improve your relationship with yourself.*
6. *As you heal, you will change. Others might not like it.*

Chapter Two:
BOUNDARIES, WANTS AND NEEDS AND ATTACHMENT STYLES

This short chapter will help to bridge your knowledge from your relationship with yourself to your relationship with others. In order to avoid too much repetition throughout the rest of the book, this chapter covers essential information around boundaries, wants and needs and attachment styles.

BOUNDARIES

Throughout this book I'll be talking a lot about boundaries. They are vital because they allow for healthy intimacy, which means you are able to learn to love both yourself and others simultaneously. Boundaries give us authority over our vulnerability, and are a fundamental ingredient to healthy relationships. Most importantly they support us in holding a healthy IWM and give us more choice over the relationships we choose to be in. They are your number one tool to feeling happier, healthier and more grounded in relationships to yourself and others because, when you can accurately sense where your boundaries are you have an internal guide as to where different relationships fit in your life.

What actually is a boundary?
I've adapted the explanations below from my first book *Your Mental Health Workout* (*YMHW*) to help fill in any gaps in your knowledge about boundaries. But ultimately I explain boundaries as a psychological mechanism that protects and contains you and other people; they help define who you are and generate intimacy in your relationships.

Internal boundaries, referred to as invisible boundaries in *YMHW*, denote the strength of self-love you hold for yourself.

You learn these from your role models. Internal or invisible boundaries help you tune into exactly who you are and stick to that, rather than attempting to define and love yourself through the eyes of others. They are an internal layer of strength that develops over time.

Generally speaking, internal boundaries are felt; others cannot see them. They support you to have faith in yourself, take care of yourself, hold on to hope, help you set limits and control what you allow into your internal experience.

External boundaries, referred to as visible boundaries in *YMHW*, are boundaries that others can see and hear. They reveal how physical you are with others and when, your personal space, what you say to others, and your sexual boundaries.

Visible boundaries protect you from shame, trauma and resentment as well as abuse and neglect in relationships outside yourself. They provide an alternative, where once you may have sacrificed parts of your own wellbeing to try and cope with what was hurting you, boundaries help you deal with what is hurting you without hurting yourself.

Boundaries can feel challenging in all types of relationships and I'd argue that the hardest relationship to maintain boundaries in is our relationship with ourselves, closely followed by family relationships. The former (self) is true because boundaries are directly linked to vulnerability, we have to be in touch with our vulnerability in order to know where we need our boundaries to be. Very often, if we lack a sense of self-worth we will struggle to hold ourselves accountable to the boundaries we set. But we can't expect others to respect our boundaries if we are not doing it for ourselves. The latter (family) is true because (1) our family relationships are where we learned about boundaries and located their whereabouts and (2) the way a family functions is usually resistant to change so it's often difficult to think about holding a boundary with a family member, never mind creating it and keeping it.

That said, your experience could be different, it would be helpful for you to take a moment now to consider which relationships you find boundaries easier and which ones require more effort from you.

How to set a boundary

Here are some simple steps, adapted from *Your Mental Health Workout* to help you set boundaries. Throughout the following four chapters boundaries will come up often, come back to these steps to help you structure and be pro-active with the information provided.

1. Identify the boundary that needs setting.
2. Imagine/visualise what it is that you would like to say or do in order to set this boundary.
3. Set the boundary.
4. Feel your feelings <u>and</u> hold the boundary.
5. Repeat as necessary.

We usually imagine setting boundaries verbally but if it feels difficult to get yourself heard you may need to be creative about how you communicate your boundary. For example: your brother may respond better to being able to read your boundary about knocking before entering. You could create a small sign for your bedroom door that reads, 'Please knock before opening the door'. With your colleague, a verbal boundary may sound more like 'I feel uncomfortable talking about that can we move on please.' Or maybe it would be better expressed in a message or email where the person can see it written down in black and white.

Boundary Backlash

Regardless of how you set a boundary, it's likely you will get a bit of boundary backlash. In other words, both you and other people are unlikely to appreciate all the feelings you get when you use a boundary, whether it's the first time or the one hundredth time. You may experience a challenging set of emotions – such as guilt, anger or sadness – and you may feel like retracting what you've said to make those feelings go away. But please ride it out, this is you holding the boundary with yourself even in the face of unpleasant backlash. The person on the receiving end of the boundary may respond with surprise, anger, condemnation or try to shame you out of the change you are creating. What they feel is more about them that it is about you.

Boundaries in healthy relationships are set with compassion and kindness. They inform other people of who you are and how to build a better bond with you and they will, in time, leave you feeling less resentful and more available to yourself and others.

WANTS AND NEEDS

Another turn of phrase you'll read about often here is 'wants and needs'. Understanding your personal wants and needs is an important part of self-connection and how you connect with others.

Needs
So that we all know what we're talking about, below is a list of your basic needs. It is heavily based on Maslow's famous hierarchy (see Further Reading), but I have unpacked some of the categories a little further so that you can check you are meeting as many of them as possible across your relationship experiences. It's your responsibility to come back to this, if you feel the need to remind yourself what your needs and wants are when I talk about them in later sections.

It's worth noting that there isn't any one relationship that can meet all of your needs but when you look at your connections as a whole, the majority of your needs should be met somewhere, either by you or by someone else.

Here is the list of your basic needs:

- Food
- Water
- Shelter
- Clothing
- Safety/Protection/Security
- Physical nurturing
- Emotional nurturing
- Medical
- Dental
- Social
- Financial
- Educational
- Sexual

Think about your current relationships and see who is meeting which need. Are there any needs that seem to be chroni-

Chapter Two: BOUNDARIES, WANTS AND NEEDS AND ATTACHMENT STYLES

cally under-addressed, or indeed over-addressed? Sometimes over-addressing one need might mean others are going under the radar.

Here are some questions to help you assess the relational needs (some of which will be met through your relationship with yourself) listed above:

- Do you give yourself affirmative messages by ensuring you are eating, sleeping and drinking enough water?
- Do you feel safe with the people you live/spend time with?
- Do you get enough hugs and physical contact?
- Do you know who to turn to when you need emotional support?
- Who supports you to take care of your physical and mental health?

Wants
Your wants are the things that make you happy in life, they are where you find your joy. Wants, in comparison to needs, are more likely to be met by you for you and can be anything you desire: material objects, holidays, experiences. Some of my wants in life are nice clothes, time to read more books, sunny beach holidays, a lovely big bookshelf to home all my books, a slightly bigger house for my family. I don't *need* any of these things but if I am getting all my needs met I can start to consider how I might make my wants a reality. And unless someone else is going to gift me any of these things (unlikely), I will need to find a way to make them happen.

Make a separate list of the things you *want* in life, things that you enjoy but are not part of your basic needs, as listed opposite.

Here are some questions to help you identify your wants:
- Where do you find joy in life?
- Are there treats and rewards you give yourself that you look forward to?
- What allows you to increase your connection to yourself?
- Are there any areas of life that you feel deprived of at the moment?

ATTACHMENT STYLES

After many years of attaching to people as a job, what I understand most about being human is that we yearn to belong – for comfort, connection and understanding. This is true for us over the entire course of our lives.

The power of comfort
In 1958 Harry Harlow started an experiment with young rhesus monkeys that provided groundbreaking empirical evidence for the importance of attachment and maternal touch in infant development. It's worth saying that these experiments would absolutely not pass an ethical board these days, but they stand as reliable and helpful research.

In Harlow's original experiment, the monkeys were separated from their mothers at birth and given two surrogate parental figures. One group of monkeys were given an uncomfortable wire mother monkey that provided food, but no comfort as well as a soft, tactile and comfy mother monkey who provided comfort but no food.

Another group of baby monkeys were given the same surrogate mothers, but the comfy monkey had food and the wire monkey did not. Without a doubt, in both of the groups, the baby monkeys bonded more with the comfy monkey. They would go to the wire monkey for food (if that's where it was) and then come straight back to comfy monkey for the majority of their time. If they were scared, they would refer to the comfy monkey regardless of what else she had to offer. The monkeys showed signs of a secure attachment with the comfy monkey and a disorganised attachment with the wire monkey.

By removing the comfy monkey, Harlow went on to show that without the experience of a secure attachment figure that could meet their needs, the young monkeys didn't really know how to relate to other monkeys. They would allow their peers to bully them, and they did not know how to be parents themselves. The monkeys self-mutilated and some died because they refused to eat. If you're interested in attachment and the biological need for connection it's worth reading more about these experiments. Just

Chapter Two: BOUNDARIES, WANTS AND NEEDS AND ATTACHMENT STYLES

search 'Harlow Monkey 1958' (or see Further Reading list). This experiment always gets me thinking about why people come to therapy. Sometimes it's to sort out their addiction, to address their negative thinking, to find their purpose in life, to explore who they are, to process their partner's affair, to seek support while dealing with being made redundant, and so on. What lies underneath many of these symptoms, as evidenced by the young monkeys who grew up to self-mutilate and refuse food, is the basic need for a comfortable place where we can be related to, be understood and be responded to in a way that allows a secure attachment to build.

Sometimes this yearning comes from things that were missed in childhood. For others the damage is done later in life via friendships, romantic attachments, workplace issues and online encounters. In my mind, people come into therapy to solve the issue in hand but also to secure someone's undivided, unjudgmental attention for a period of time, something we rarely find in our day-to-day relationships.

So, what are attachment styles?

Attachment styles are patterns of bonding, usually instilled in childhood and carried forward into adulthood. As their name suggests, they quite literally refer to how we psychologically and emotionally attach to others and the effects these attachments have on our behaviour. Although most attachment research is done with children and caregivers it is relevant throughout our lives as we form attachments with all sorts of different people. I also believe that our attachment styles can change over time, if we want them to.

Having an idea of how you attach to specific types of people will support you to change if you want. But it will also prepare you, protect you and most importantly support you to have compassion for yourself in times when relationships feel like they need a bit of hard work put into them.

What kind of attachment styles are there?

The healthiest type of attachment style is called a 'secure attachment'. A secure attachment means that you feel a proportionate amount of distress when your attachment figure leaves, but you retain a sense that they will always come back to you, and that they will be there if you need them.

When your secure attachment figure is present you feel safe, seen, soothed and secure (see *The Power of Showing Up* in Further Reading). Experiments with young children have shown that a child with a secure attachment will play independently while their attachment figure is present. They intermittently return to their caregiver to 'check in' and then continue with their independent play. We do this 'checking in' with our attachment figures as adults too, but in a more sophisticated way. It's easier to notice our 'checking in' behaviours when we are feeling a little vulnerable or anxious – maybe you text your parent, partner or close friends more often and feel the need to be physically closer to them – this is evidence of a secure attachment.

There are also a set of 'insecure' attachment styles, but that doesn't mean they are a bad thing, as all attachment styles are about how we relate to others and manage to stay in relationships.

Usually, an insecure attachment style is born out of how we were related to as children and what nurture and comfort was made available to us. Through this, as you know from the previous chapter, we learn about relational safety and healthy intimacy, and we carry forward what we are taught in life.

Below is a very short description of how insecure attachments might show up in adulthood:

- **Preoccupied or anxious attachments** – With this attachment style you may find yourself chronically craving intimacy, feeling needy and dependent on others. You may find yourself hooked on thinking about others and acting in ways you imagine might mean you get approval from them. You often project magical qualities on to others and place them on a pedestal – this is actually a way of trying to soothe your anxiety within the relationship.
- **Dismissive or avoidant attachments** – This attachment style is characterised by a stubborn form of self-sufficiency. You may struggle to let others help you and guard yourself against intimacy. You might appear uninterested, as if you do not care about relationships. Deep down you fear rejection and abandonment so much that you'd rather not risk it at all.

Chapter Two: BOUNDARIES, WANTS AND NEEDS AND ATTACHMENT STYLES

- **Fearful or disorganised attachments** – This attachment style is characterised by the suffering caused by an internal conflict that simultaneously craves close relationships and fears the intimacy and vulnerability that's involved. It often involves an attitude of 'Go away, don't leave me!'. Often there is no consistent pattern within a disorganised attachment style.

What is my attachment style?
Do any of the above descriptions remind you of parts of yourself? Maybe you fit into one or all of the definitions. Although many of us have an attachment style we default to most often, you don't need to pigeonhole yourself into one category or the other. In my experience it's worth keeping an open mind and observing your thoughts, feelings and behaviours related to attachment across all your relationships rather than assuming you always attach in one way or another.

Chapter Three:
FAMILY RELATIONSHIPS

Reflective question: 'How would relationships be different for you if you'd had an entirely "functional" family?'

This chapter will probably have the most impact on helping you understand why you choose the people you choose and how to change that pattern, if you want to. What you discover should make it much easier to understand your friendships, romantic patterns, workplace relationships and online behaviours. I hope to offer you a solid understanding of how the hallmark of your specific family system, functional or otherwise, affects all your other relationships.

WHAT IS A FAMILY?

A small warning to help you manage your expectations, I am not going to tell you how to speak to your father or how to mend that sibling rift. It would be impossible for me to stipulate a course of action that would work for everyone who reads this. You are all individuals, and your family hallmarks are like fingerprints: no two are the same. Instead, we will be working towards understanding your unique family dynamic and the part you play in it, building on all you gained in the previous section. Through that knowledge you should start to feel more capable of change within yourself and therefore gradually notice improvements in your family relationships.

Family of Origin (FOO)
Your Family Of Origin (FOO) is the group of people you were born into, or your significant caregivers. They do not have to be related to you by blood or marriage, but they need to have featured considerably in your care as a child. I use the FOO concept to avoid the heteronormative idea of a nuclear family, which has traditionally been defined by two parents and their children related by blood or marriage and living in the same household. This is a good defi-

Chapter Three: FAMILY RELATIONSHIPS

nition of the word 'family', for those who the term still fits. But blended and chosen families are many people's reality, and using the term FOO means, for the sake of this book, that any combination of familiar relationship fits our definition and therefore what we mean by 'family'.

To my knowledge, American psychiatrist and professor Murray Bowen came up with the idea of FOO in 1950, and since then many others have used it to develop therapy models that help us work on our family relationships. His pioneering work on family therapy, created the notion of the family system that psychology refers to so often. He also established the idea of *systemic therapy*, a non-analytical type of therapy that explores relationships in groups, such as our families, by exploring the patterns and dynamics we play out. These theories are now taught in the majority of psychology and psychotherapy qualifications and training courses.

In the late 1980s, Pia Mellody, a pioneer in **co-dependent** recovery, used a similar concept to create a trauma reduction and **re-parenting** model based around the idea of FOO that helps clients to undertake an in-depth review of how family relationships and systems can impair our growth and development. It's called Post Induction Therapy (PIT). It's the inner child model I alluded to in Chapter One. I trained in PIT in 2014 and to this day I use its approach to support my clients in understanding their FOO and release themselves from relational trauma.

In order to help you understand the hallmark your FOO has created for you, we will need to explore the history of your family relationships – the healthy and the less healthy. To do this I am going to give you a lot of information about family systems, and it's your job to decide which bits you relate to and which bits you don't as well as potentially which bits I've missed. The exercises may bring up feelings from your childhood and although I am okay with you experiencing your emotions and expanding your *window of tolerance* as you do this work, I have no interest in destabilising you or any area of your life. I would strongly suggest you start a journal so you have somewhere to process the messy emotions that may surface. Often being able to simply get them out of your mind helps you feel less alone, more contained, more understanding and most importantly, safer. A journal would be particularly helpful if you are not currently in therapy. If you do find yourself feeling unsafe and destabilised, please see pages 226-227 for guidance on how to seek further support.

A note to parents
When I became a parent, I found myself applying the concepts of Pia Mellody's PIT model in real time, in an effort to pass down healing rather than trauma to my *family of creation*. I gravitated towards the concept of gentle parenting and raising children with dignity and respect. Which basically means endeavouring to treat their feelings, views, needs and wants as seriously as I would treat those of an adult.

Pia Mellody's model, along with other models, and much of what I write here, has been created to heal adults who were not raised as gently and kindly as many parents are raising their children today. To be clear, gentle parenting is not about letting kids do whatever they want without the necessary boundaries; it means setting the boundaries, rules, expectations and consequences out of love rather than punishment and working as a team rather than engaging in *power dynamics*.

I'm hopeful that a revolution of gentle parenting is starting. One where we start by re-parenting ourselves in a kind and gentle way and follow suit by treating our children as equals so that they grow up with a healthy understanding and attitude towards all relationships, and a sense of inherent self-worth less fragile than the generation before them.

The truth is, most of the parenting advice that was given to our parents and grandparents was put into books by white, middle-aged men. That advice has now been shown to actively work against relational and biological needs such as physical contact, intuitive eating and empathy within relationships. Remember the monkeys? They chose comfort every time... even over food. Is it any wonder that so many of us seek support to help us circumnavigate relationships when we were potentially parented or at least disciplined in a way that bypassed some of our most basic needs?

If you happen to be a parent, or are about to become one, and you want to raise your children with dignity and respect, I am hopeful that what I share in this section will support you to heal your

Chapter Three: FAMILY RELATIONSHIPS

FOO relationships and do things differently with your family of creation (see also the titles in the Further Reading section by Sarah Ockwell-Smith). As you learn, you may start to worry about the impact you have already had on your children. Please try and keep your focus on your experience of your Family Of Origin rather than your Family of Creation (FOC). If you heal your FOO wounds your FOC will automatically be a happier and healthier place to be.

Side note: Your family relationships may not be entirely dysfunctional. They may be very functional and happy in parts, but no one seeks support because they want to talk about how authentically functional and happy their family is. So we'll be focusing on the parts that might need tweaking. I always keep in mind that most people will also have lots of positive and helpful experiences within their FOO.

Exercise: How did/do you feel about your significant caregivers?

Make a list of all the significant caregivers from your childhood. Write down how you felt about them when you were a child, and how you feel looking back on your relationship with them now.

BUT I HAD A REALLY HAPPY CHILDHOOD...

I've had many a client who, when I start asking about their FOO, tell me that they had a very happy childhood, that there are zero significant events to recall that could justify why they find romantic relationships challenging or why they guard themselves in friendships and do not let anyone get too close to them. They tell me that their childhood is not the reason they've come to therapy. I also have clients who've come to therapy because they have significant issues within their family relationships and therefore relational childhood trauma plays a conscious function in their lives. For any of these clients, it is often tough to talk about family history because they haven't made the necessary connections to understand the full effect of family relationships on them... yet. Whichever category you fall into, we will be working together to help you do exactly that in this chapter.

The majority of us are born directly into relationships with our FOO. Others who may have been adopted or fostered may not have been born into their FOO, but these early and hopefully long-term relationships constitute a FOO. Regardless, we are primed to need to be connected, accepted, approved of and loved by them. We need to feel we belong in our FOO; therefore, we can have some very deep, complex and at times painful experiences within our family relationships alongside the joyous, happy and wonderful ones.

We sometimes develop behaviours that disguise the pain we feel in our family relationships, possibly to try and hold on to the idea of a happy childhood and possibly to try and separate from it. My attempt at this was my eating disorder. My disordered eating was far easier to discuss in therapy than the pain I felt in my relationships with my family, specifically my relationship with my mother. Once I got into recovery around food, I realised that I would probably spend, well... the rest of my life, trying to untangle and comprehend my relationship with my mum. Likewise, when I am working with a client and we get to the difficulties they have had in relation to (usually) their same-sex parent, I know we are working at the core of the issue, regardless of their reports of a happy or unhappy childhood.

It's the core of the issue because, in heterosexual couples, generally speaking, the same-sex parent is our model for how we relate to ourselves, whereas the opposite-sex parent is our model for how we relate to others. Understandably, this can look a bit different when there are different sexualities and gender identities in the mix. For example, a pair of same-sex parents would model the same pattern, but the children may take masculine and feminine traits from one or both parents, or choose to identify with one parent over the other regardless of gender identity. When parents identify with more fluid gender roles, fluidity will also be present in the children as they learn and grow in their relationships with themselves and others.

Our emotional investment in family relationships is complex and challenging to untangle particularly if you perceive your childhood to be a very happy one. It often feels easier to focus on the catalyst

Chapter Three: FAMILY RELATIONSHIPS

that prompted you to seek therapy or pick up this book, rather than on the underlying cause. The symptom might be something like an addiction, relationship difficulties, or a chronic feeling that you lack purpose in life. Maybe you have been single for ten years and can't figure out why, but the truth of the matter is that you HAVE to get underneath the symptom to understand why you are really seeking help.

As we explored in the previous chapter, the people who raise us have a momentous influence on who we become, how we regulate ourselves and how we feel about ourselves. Their psychological support informs our self-worth, where our boundaries are, and how we implement them – as well as how capably we can represent our realities and indeed build bonds with people outside our families. Our FOO profoundly informs who we go on to have other relationships with, which is why, even if you had a very happy, carefree childhood we need to explore it.

Examples of how family relationships impact us elsewhere
Here are two really short and hopefully helpful examples of why family relationships need to be explored and worked on:

A chronic feeling that you lack purpose in life (as mentioned above) may feel like it stems from not feeling respected or driven in your workplace, but when we dig a little further we find that not feeling respected is a *familiar* experience for you because, even if your childhood was on the whole a wonderful one, if your father (as an example) didn't feel respected throughout his own life, therefore couldn't model respect by respecting you, you may find yourself in positions and dynamics as an adult that provoke the same feelings. We repeat what we don't repair.

The same would be true if you had a highly critical parent. As you enter the world of relationships outside your FOO you may find yourself feeling criticised everywhere you go. It is of course simply not possible for *everyone* to be criticising you – this is in fact a way of imagining yourself at the centre of everyone else's thoughts (that's a hard one to hear I know). You've internalised your highly critical parent and are *projecting* your experience on to others. Even as an adult you are being internally parented by the unhelpful parent you once knew.

In both these examples we can see how familiar experiences are being projected on to other areas in life and affecting other relationships negatively. If you want to achieve authentic intimacy with people, you need to know, firstly, when you are projecting experiences from your original family system onto relationships outside your FOO, and then, how to change it, if you want to. One of the main factors in healthy relationships, with anyone, is being able to be present and responding to the other person as they are, not as you perceive them based on your history or the current state you are moving through.

As we start to delve into this, it's important to remember that, as per the example above, your father likely didn't show you an absence of respect intentionally; your parent probably didn't realise how critical they were being. They were, most likely, doing the very best version of parenting they had available to them. What they are showing you, somewhat sadly, is how they were parented, the emotions they are carrying, and the damage they have not yet healed from.

Exercise: Journal Opportunity

Imagine yourself as a child. What did you need from your caregivers that you didn't get? Or didn't get enough of?

TRANSGENERATIONAL TRAUMA

To understand more deeply the impact your family hallmark has on you, it can also be valuable to look beyond your FOO and explore what is being passed down your bloodline from previous generations. There will be lots of positive things you have inherited from your grandparents and great-grandparents and there will also be transgenerational trauma – until someone can prove otherwise, I believe there is transgenerational trauma in everyone's family.

Certain terminology around trauma seems to go in and out of fashion. The term 'big T trauma, little t trauma' was fashionable for a while and it referred to the difference between major traumatic

Chapter Three: FAMILY RELATIONSHIPS

events like accidents, rape and abuse (big T), and the smaller things that can also damage us – like having an unavailable parent or being exposed to family ruptures without witnessing the repair (little t). Arguably, large clusters of little t trauma can be harder to heal from than one big T trauma, but I'll leave you to make your own mind up about that.

When I talk about trauma, I am referring to anything that was less than helpful in your life, also known as an adverse life experience – anything that had enough of an impact on your internal world that you experience a flight, fight, freeze or fawn response (the four different types of trauma responses) whenever you are reminded of it. In the words of physician Gabor Maté, 'Trauma is not what happens to you...it is what happens inside you as a result of what happened to you'.

Types of Trauma Response
The 'fight or flight response' is a term coined in 1926 by Walter Cannon, an American physiologist, professor and the then-chairman at Harvard Medical School (see Further Reading). Over the years the 'freeze' and 'fawn' responses have been added by other professionals to help explain the state of hyperarousal that occurs when we are having an acute stress response. In the context of relational trauma, transgenerational or otherwise, fight, flight, freeze and fawn responses may look like this:

FLIGHT response can be quite literally running away, leaving a situation, panicking or escaping. Escape can also happen in your mind in the form of fantasising about something that makes you feel better. It might mean you literally say you need to leave very suddenly and scurry off when triggered, but it could also be much more subtle, for example: an anxious bladder that makes you leave a situation to 'go to the toilet' when your trauma is activated. (Note: If you have an anxious bladder, you really *will* go to the toilet when this happens so it can be hard to spot. If this is relevant to you: each time you leave a situation to go to the toilet, start being mindful of what was happening just before and how you felt.)

FIGHT response is, you guessed it, fighting back. This can include exploding, shouting, insulting, humiliating, blaming, shaming, raging, physical aggression or passive aggression. You may not always exhibit these behaviours externally; you could have rage fantasies or feel the fight response kick in internally instead.

FREEZE response may show itself as going silent, losing your words, not being able to think straight, or ***dissociation***. It is effectively 'playing dead', as an animal in the wild would do if a predator got too close. The difference between us and a wild animal is that the animal naturally, once the threat has passed, gets up, shakes out all the adrenaline and cortisol that the nervous system releases when it percieves a threat and carries on with its day, reducing the acute stress response. Human beings, these days, lead a much more sedentary lifestyle and rather than allowing the body to process what has happened through movement or allowing the emotion to come up via having a cry to release some of the overload of cortisol, we tend to repress and store the experience. This can lead to things like insomnia or sleeping difficulties, physical issues, burnout and anxiety and depression.

FAWN response is when you become submissive, and tolerate far more than is appropriate or realistic. We are driven to gain love and acceptance from our caregivers and close family members at all costs, even in the face of a traumatic relationship experience. I cannot tell you how common this response is within family relationships. People pleasing (see p. 73-5) and compulsive helping (p. 75-6) fall into the fawn category. You may use people pleasing and compulsive helping behaviours to try to gain approval from the relationship that has activated your fawn response through placation.

How do I know if I am carrying trauma?

There are two parts to carried trauma: transgenerational trauma and carried emotion. Although they are slightly different to each other, they often get grouped together, and I have done so here because there are so many crossovers.

Carried emotion can be less about a traumatic event and more about who's taking responsibility for the lasting emotional impact, hence the use of the word emotion. The term literally means that some of the thoughts, feelings and behaviours we engage with are carried through family relationships via people's unconscious or conscious behaviours towards each other, rather than being ex-

Chapter Three: FAMILY RELATIONSHIPS

perienced first-hand. This works in opposition too; we can carry positive experiences, but we tend not to focus on them as they do not show up as issues in relationships or contribute to mental health problems.

The clearest example of carried emotion I can give is when someone, usually a parent, shames and blames family members rather than taking responsibility for their part in what's happening. They are discharging their emotions on to others to make themselves feel better and other people feel worse. The other person feels worse because they are now carrying the emotion. People may do this due to 'Big T' transgenerational trauma, or because they have not been shown how to take responsibility for their own feelings, which could be thought of as 'little t' trauma.

Transgenerational trauma, at the risk of repeating myself, is more concentrated on specific traumas that family members have been through, and can be traced back as far as seven generations. Transgenerational trauma usually involves some level of carried emotion. When I am involved with a client in trauma reduction work, which will almost certainly entail releasing carried shame, anger, sadness, depression, anxiety, I am aware, and want to help them understand, that their experience could be connected to something a family member went through a very long time ago. The client, in the chair in front of me (or next to me as is the case when we do trauma reduction work), may have no idea what led to their using anorexia as a way of regulating emotion (as an example) but their great-great-grandparent who was in a camp at Auschwitz might be able to explain a feeling of being punished and starved of food and water just for being who they were and for holding a particular belief system. The shame that comes with being treated like this gets carried forward and passed onto others through unhealthy relational behaviours, because it's too painful for the person who experiences it first hand to face and heal from. Previous generations have not had the opportunity or awareness to heal themselves in the same way we do now. To take the example of my client with anorexia, they are living with symptoms of trauma and carried emotion that were created long before they were even born.

It's beneficial to practice differentiating which of your experiences are carried (trauma, emotion or both), and which are your own.

When you carry something for a family member you can end up taking responsibility for it without knowing why, which means the other person does not have to. So my client in the above example is responsible for their recovery from anorexia, but it may help them to know that their difficulties are a response to trauma that wasn't theirs to cope with in the first place. The process of 'handing back' feelings of shame and torture, even to relatives that are no longer with us, can help release people from the grips of a disease like anorexia.

You can apply this to yourself by thinking of a time when you took responsibility for something that wasn't yours to take, maybe at work or in your friendship group. Do you remember how you felt? Most likely, on some level, you felt resentful. When we carry experiences for family members, we can end up unconsciously (or indeed consciously) resenting them, which may show up, if the family member is still alive during your lifetime, as a 'difficult' relationship, or a feeling of anger or even hate towards a family member.

If an experience isn't carried, generally you'll find that your response is contextual to the situation and other people will advocate for that. You'll also find it easier to let things go once you've said or done what you feel needs to be done. And there are times when it's more complex than that too, we can experience a contextual reaction and have carried emotion or trauma attached to it. Awareness is key and as you mature into this work you will be able to separate the two and work on both things in tandem.

A bit of science, for those of you who want the hard and fast research

Over the past 20 years new research has proven that the idea of transgenerational trauma and carried emotion is not just something made up by old-school therapists, it is absolutely a scientific thing. In fact, not only is it a psychological and social science, it's also a biological phenomenon that now has a name: epigenetics.

Epigenetics is the study of how life events and your environment affect your DNA and how these changes are carried through generations.

This vital research, along with research on *neuroplasticity*, backs up the anecdotal therapeutic evidence we've had for decades that people can change within themselves, change who they are attracted to, change their attachment styles and recover from traumatic events, even if the event is carried.

To summarise: when trauma happens it can be carried through families, but there is no actual change to your genetic code. Instead, disturbances happen that impact tiny and specific parts of your genes, but they can be stripped back, removed, or 'switched off' as many trauma therapists would put it, to reveal an entirely healthy set of DNA.

My client with anorexia is a great example. Their great-grandparent suffered stressful and traumatic events that had biological consequences resulting in long-lasting after-effects. These biological changes mean my client has inherited a predisposition to food restriction, but it is not who they are destined to be. It is not written in their DNA – it's a disturbance they carry. For the restrictive behaviour to be activated, there also needs to be a stressful or traumatic life event that my client must somehow cope with and a social group (which can be family) that tolerates the behaviour. The magic is that, if they find authentic and sustained recovery and freedom from food restriction, they will, hopefully, not pass it on to the next generation, if they choose to procreate.

If you're struggling with an eating disorder of any kind and would like help, please see pages 226-227 for some guidance on where to find support.

Exercise: Identifying Carried Experiences

Take some time over the next few days to observe the way you think, feel and behave in your relationship to family members. Although it can highlight things more easily, you don't need to be with them in person to do this.

Observe any feelings, thoughts or behaviours with no apparent roots in your lived experience. For example, are you highly anxious without a known cause? Do you carry financial or sexual shame and don't really know why?

BUILDING BONDS

> *Start making a list, somewhere private, of the experiences you think you might be carrying for someone else in your family. You can simply continue to observe and come to your own conclusions about it, or you can take the content to therapy if that feels helpful.*

Reminder: This is not a blaming exercise, this is your chance to practise being brutally honest with yourself (see Chapter One), represent your experiences accurately, and create a space where you're able to accept the responsibility that is yours for the necessary in your family relationships, and give back any responsibility that belongs to others. **Do not take this exercise to the family member in question as it may disempower you.** Later, we will uncover some strategies to support you in building healthier connections and talking about some of this material. If difficult feelings are triggered, please write them down in your journal and speak to your therapist or counsellor (if you have one) or a trusted friend if you need to.

FAMILY ROLES

Family roles are the repeated behaviours and dynamics that make your family function, for better or worse. The top layer of family roles is an easy one. You're a sister, mother, uncle, brother, grandparent, nephew, and so on, and you hold the responsibilities that come with that title in your unique family system.

The next layer is a bit harder to determine because it's less about responsibilities and much more about how each of you secures love, connection, approval and attention. These roles may show up in a healthy family system, but are most commonly acknowledged within dysfunctional family relationships. Austrian psychoanalyst, Alfred Alder's conceptualisation of what we now call Birth Theory outlines the charactistics in each family role. In fact he was the first person to predict that our position in our family could dictate behaviour and personality traits (there are books and information online that expand further on this; I've included a book I particularly like by Tian Dayton in the Further Reading section). Categorised by author and counsellor Sharon Wegscheider-Cruse, they are hero,

Chapter Three: FAMILY RELATIONSHIPS

mascot, scapegoat, enabler, rescuer, and the lost child. Below, I've given a brief outline for each. Please note these are most relevant in families where issues are present; however, whether you do or don't want to start opening up new conversations, it's fundamental to you gaining choice within your relationships that you are aware of the roles you play. It is also important to have some self-awareness about which roles you tend to fall into, so that you can build healthier and more intimate relationships within your family and beyond.

HERO – Often the first born, the Hero in the family might be a high-achiever, chronically self-reliant, a perfectionist, a problem solver and also anxious, lonely and insecure. They come across as 'mature for their age'. Their job is to maintain the 'perfect' picture of a functional family (even if that's not the case). They often carry the family secrets and issues and tend to align their views and opinions with the parent group in order to gain approval. Alder considered the first born to be the more neurotic one in the birth order.

SCAPEGOAT – Often the second born, the Scapegoat appears to be the opposite of the Hero. The family member who takes on the scapegoat role will often 'rebel' and 'act out' in order to express themselves. They struggle with boundaries and can appear chaotic and uncontained. They are named as the 'problem' in the family and tend to come under more criticism than other siblings as a bias towards blaming them develops. But really... they come into an already formed family unit (caregivers and first born) where the love and attention for being a 'hero' is already taken, so they need to carve out a different type of attention. They secure an alternative type of love by behaving in a different way. On the more positive side of things, they also tend to be more sociable and friendly than the Hero or first born child.

LOST CHILD – Often the third or final sibling in a family, born within five years of the second-youngest sibling, the Lost Child finds themselves ignored and their needs and wants left unattended. This leads the individual to shut down on their need for connection and relationship. Alder described this person as affectionate and uncomplicated, although they can also be quite manipulative at times. In some ways, whether in family or individual therapy, this is the family member I'd feel most concerned about. They often slide under the radar and are prone to problems like depression, self-harm, screen addiction and suicidal ideation.

MASCOT – The Mascot in the family (also a role that the third born often assumes) plays the joker or the clown. They are the person who breaks the ice with their wit in order to distract from tension and conflict. The Mascot's job is to try to cover up the family pain and dysfunction. People who play the Mascot role may come across as quite immature and inside feel powerless and lost as to how to navigate life.

ENABLER or RESCUER – Often a parent but not always, the Enabler or Rescuer appears caring and helpful, but in fact enables all other dysfunctional family roles. They will often make excuses for unacceptable behaviour and step in to 'fix things', therefore allowing others to avoid taking responsibility for unhealthy behaviours and patterns. This person may experience very high levels of anxiety, anger and even panic attacks if their help is not well received. They need people to need them and cannot tolerate the messiness of others experiencing the consequences of their own behaviours.

And yes, you can spend time in all of these roles at different points in your life and in relation to different family members as well as transferring the behaviours onto the relationships outside the FOO. You might be a Lost Child in relation to your mother but a Scapegoat in relation to your father and anyone who reminds you of your caregivers may trigger you in these roles and behaviours. Although the original literature is quite prescriptive in terms of birth order and who plays what role, I've learned over the years that people's experiences of these roles often differs, depending on the state of health or dysfunction the family is experiencing at any time.

If you happen to be an only child, you may find yourself wondering how you fit into all this... how many of these roles can you identify with? The likelihood is that as an only child you are most vulnerable to slipping into different roles at different times and with different people. You'll be a master at being all things to all people to try and get your connection and approval needs met.

Although there are times in our lives when it is appropriate to step into these roles, when we are playing them out unconsciously as a substitute for authentic and unconditional love, they tend to cause disharmony in our lives. When you are able to identify which role you are slipping into and with whom, you are then granted the choice as to whether you'd be happy to continue playing that role, or if it is causing you pain enough to change. See the table below to get an idea of the changes that are available to you.

Exercise: Family Roles

Which of the roles above do you identify with? You may identify with all of them at different points in your life and with different people in your family, or maybe there is one consistent role you feel you've always played.

Take it Further
Can you identify any of your family members in the roles above? We're not here to take their inventory, but reflecting on the question might help you form a more solid understanding of yourself.

How would you like things to be different?

Recovery options for family roles that no longer serve you
This is by no means a complete list of recovery options, just some gentle ideas about where you might like to start to make some changes.

Family Role	Old behaviour	Suggestions for new behaviour
Hero	Feels that they have to be the best and impress people. High achiever, self-reliant, keeps secrets and feelings hidden behind a 'perfect' mask.	Work on your self-esteem and accept being good enough and equal to others, rather than better than and perfect. Practise asking for help and telling the truth about how you feel.

BUILDING BONDS

Scapegoat	Feels, and is often told, that they are the problem. Is both given and takes the blame for things, struggles with boundaries and self-esteem.	Work on your boundaries both internal and external. Notice when you cross others' boundaries and also what boundaries you might need in place to protect yourself from carrying other people's issues in your family.
Mascot	Feels powerless to change things. Makes jokes to disguise pain. Allows people to laugh at, or with, them if it defuses conflict and avoids difficulty, but this has a negative impact on their self-esteem and indicates a lack of personal boundaries.	Work on tolerating the uncomfortable tension that comes in all families at times. Practise sitting with silence for a bit and pause to consider how you are feeling and reacting before cracking a joke or saying something witty to deflect from difficulty and conflict. Work on your internal and external boundaries.
Lost Child	Feels lost and unnoticed. Out of touch with wants and needs. Often anxious and/or depressed.	Work on reconnecting with your wants and needs and then practise asking for them to be met. You will feel fear when you do this, so please do it with people who you think will be receptive.
Enabler/ Rescuer	Feels they need to fix others, often tries to placate issues, and might use things like money or compulsive helping to avoid conflict and chaos. This means that others do not have an opportunity to learn from the consequences of their behaviour.	Work on letting your family members take responsibility for their emotions and behaviours. Start stepping back and allowing space for others to make mistakes and learn from the consequences.

Chapter Three: FAMILY RELATIONSHIPS

IDENTIFYING HEALTHY OR FUNCTIONAL PARTS OF A FAMILY SYSTEM

So far, we've looked at the parts of your family that may need improving or could be labelled dysfunctional, and I've already mentioned healthy and unhealthy family systems without fully explaining what these may look like. It is very possible that your family has entirely functional behaviours in some departments and not so functional in others. Like most things in life, it's a spectrum and we have to understand both ends of the spectrum in order to place ourselves on it.

I believe that a healthy family is one that recognises rather than denies any issues and is equipped with the tools to cope with and navigate those issues. Put differently, healthy families are healthy because of how they navigate difficulty rather than the avoidance or absence of it. This is exactly why the roles detailed above, seemingly more evident in unhealthy set-ups may also, at times, show up even in the most functional of families.

Although I am going to continue to use the terms, just for sake of ease, if you'd prefer not to label yours or anyone else's family system as healthy or unhealthy, we take the judgement out of this thinking in the following exercise, by considering the characteristics within your family, as these make up your family hallmark.

Your Family Hallmark

Think through your experience in your family. Can you describe your family hallmark without judging it as good or bad, healthy or unhealthy?
 For example:
 'In my family we look after each other with actions such as being available for get togethers and helping each other out a lot rather than saying words such as "I love you".' 'In my family we've navigated addiction and depression by supporting each other.'
 'My family are always/sometimes/never available for me when I need them.'

The following list might help you advance your thinking around this.

Three things healthy/functional families do:

1. They respect each other's individuality.
   Healthy families are neither enmeshed nor isolated from each other. They understand that each person is a separate being with individual wants and needs, goals and desires in life. And that every individual has a set of love and connection wants and needs that should be met within the family.

2. They use boundaries out of love.
   Healthy families are able to explain, express and understand that boundaries come from a place of love, not one of criticism and punishment. They do not use boundaries, rules, power or authority to provoke, discipline or punish each other.

3. They feel safe with each other.
   Each family member feels safe within the family system. They feel safe enough to ask for help, have their needs met and make mistakes. They do not fear being told off, rejected or disapproved of when they are honest about their experiences, reality, feelings or thoughts.

You might look at this list and think the word 'communication' is missing. This is a deliberate omission, as is the word 'co-regulation' (which we covered on p. 19). Many families think they communicate well, because they talk to each other frequently and articulately, but if the three points above are not being met, the connection and co-regulation piece that makes a healthy family system is still missing.

Exercise: An opportunity to Reflect

Your family may engage in some, all or none of the list above. Take a moment now to consider which functional behaviours are present. Reflect on what your ideal, healthy family would look like.

Chapter Three: FAMILY RELATIONSHIPS

Take it Further
Journal on the heathy part of your family system. Are there ways of being that you would like to take forward in life? Who taught you them? Be specific, give examples.

IDENTIFYING UNHEALTHY PARTS OF A FAMILY SYSTEM

The following sections aim to help you to become aware of and identify specific behaviours towards the unhealthy or dysfunctional end of the spectrum in your family.

We've already covered some of what an unhealthy family system involves when we explored the different family roles. These roles are often, but not always, attributed to the children in the family. Some of you may not like what I am about to say, some of you may think it's a strikingly obvious thing to point out and some of you may prefer to think that this is a subjective issue; an unhealthy or dysfunctional family system starts with the parents. As you will have gathered from all you've read so far, there are numerous layers to this statement and for the sake of keeping it as simple as possible we will look at how you can identify healthy or unhealthy patterns in your immediate family system – for both caregivers and child(ren).

In psychology, to help us categorise things, we refer to the parents as the 'parent group', and the children as the 'sibling group' – or if you're an only child we'll simply use the term 'only child'. Often dysfunction is attributed to the sibling group/only child as they might be the ones fighting with each other or behaving in other ways that suggest a level of emotional dysregulation. This is sometimes referred to as 'acting out' or 'rebelling', and is not unhealthy. But, if the children are doing their best to cope with the emotions and behaviours that the adults around them are not taking responsibility for, and they're coping by unconsciously mirroring back what they are observing and learning, what is actually happening with the children is simply a reflection of the unspoken and undealt with issues in the parent group. The children are absorbing the parents' dysfunction that they may then carry forward in their lives. The children get labelled as the 'issue', but the solution lies with the parents.

An example: I worked with a client whose family tragically lost a child in a freak accident. Before the accident she remembers her family life to be perfectly happy, after the accident everything changed. When her brother died, she also lost her parents to their all-consuming grief. When we explored what had gone on at home after the loss of her sibling, it became clear that the loss was never discussed, never processed. The parents' relationship broke down and everyone grieved in silence in their own way. My client learned to cut off from her emotions and 'not care' about anyone. This defence and the rest of the behaviours that the siblings displayed were not unhealthy in their own right, in fact you could consider them very resourceful coping mechanisms, but the way the parents dealt, or did not deal with the grief that followed was unhealthy (granted they likely did not know how to work through the devastation they were feeling themselves never mind support their kids). Yet, it's the kids who are in therapy trying to work out what happened to them. My client did exceedingly well in life but has struggled in romantic relationships and held onto few friendships. Now in her mid-forties she is trying to commit to someone and finds it agonizingly painful, partly because the trauma and the defences she carries has attracted someone whose unresolved issues reflect their own.

Children are like sponges, they absorb everything (information, behaviours, feelings) and if they do not find a way to discharge the energies they've been exposed to, they will end up carrying and repeating what their parents could not take responsibility for.

A family is healthy if the parents can try to understand where 'unhealthy' behaviour is coming from and look at their part in it. Sadly, children are often punished for being chaotic, dysregulated and un-boundaried (which most of the time is either developmentally appropriate or because they lack models around healthy boundaries) and therefore they end up carrying the emotions which parents are not taking responsibility for. Common examples that often show up in therapy are carried anger, shame, sadness, grief and fear.

What happens next is that the child(ren) is (are) scapegoated for their behaviour. They become the focus, and the parent is, in effect, let off the hook. In my opinion, this is the foremost observable dynamic of an unhealthy family system and it's easy to spot because

Chapter Three: FAMILY RELATIONSHIPS

everyone is pointing their finger at the person who is misbehaving, unable to control their emotional responses and struggling with their mental health, or for whom life always seems difficult. Pointing the finger and focusing on the Scapegoat means the rest of the family do not have to take accountability for their own dysfunction, which will include any relational trauma from their history and the roles they tend to play. If someone is being scapegoated, by definition, the other members in the family will be playing out other family roles.

It's sometimes believed that the members of a family who develop the most problematic symptoms and experience a level of pain that forces them to change are the same ones who can break down the denial that maintains their family's dysfunction – *if* the other family members become willing to do their work too. Consequently, as much as the 'identified patient' may be portrayed as a lost cause, they can in fact be a very powerful force for change within any family system, moving the whole system from the dysfunctional end of the spectrum closer to the functional end.

Whether or not you can pursue this work with family members on board, please know that it's very normal to stray back into FOO problems that you're trying to escape when you attempt to relate to family members again. This is mainly because family members have often witnessed the most vulnerable parts of you, and those parts will pretty much always want to be seen, understood, accepted and loved by these people, so it's totally normal to regress in their presence, and you will build resilience over time as your relationship with yourself continues to improve.

The exception here is in family relationships that are strained, toxic or abusive. I hesitate to label these exceptions as our need to be seen, understood, accepted and loved can still be true even in the worst-case scenarios…

Reminder: *you don't NEED your family to do this work at the same time as you, for you to start developing a more nourishing relationship with them. Working on your self-development isn't, or at least shouldn't be, dependent on other people coming along for the ride. So even if you're reading this and thinking that there's no point unless the rest of the family get on board, give yourself the gift of hope* *(see pp. 11-14) and be reminded that this is still about you.*

If your family jump on board with you now, sooner, or later ... then great, but please don't restrict your application of what you read in this book to be conditional on other people. You can start making the changes available to you now and work on your communication skills while letting go of the conditions and expectations that others will do the same.

TOXIC FAMILY MEMBERS, STRAINED RELATIONSHIPS AND ABUSE

We can use all sorts of words to describe a relationship that we would most likely put at the unhealthy end of the spectrum and shouldn't continue with because it has ongoing negative consequences on us. For the sake of this book, I have split the relationships that fit into this end of the spectrum into 'strained', 'toxic' and 'abusive' and defined them in my own words below. It's important to know the difference as we are never really objective in relation to family members, due to our biological need to be accepted by them.

Strained family relationships usually require you to work on your boundaries so you can support yourself in holding on to your self-esteem and self-worth. A strained relationship might be one that feels hard and uncomfortable but affects you less negatively than an abusive or toxic relationship, on the whole.

Toxic family members are the ones who defy all attempts to maintain the three points I listed earlier that help create a healthy family system (pp. 65-7): a sense of respect, boundaries and safety. Toxicity, in adult relationships, is however a dynamic – it's what happens to you in relation to that family member, how you receive them and how you feel around them. I don't think it's always fair to label individuals as toxic (as it's a judgement), but if their effect on your life is toxic, then you have a right to acknowledge your adult reality within that relationship.

Abusive family members are the ones who are objectively harming you through some means. Occasionally, abusive family members are very easy to spot: they are abusive in one or more ways. At other times, abuse can be more covert (see the table in the next subsection on page 72).

Chapter Three: FAMILY RELATIONSHIPS

With all of the above, as adults we have the power to change things. It feels hard because it's very likely that you've been in this relationship since you were a child, and the child part of you is still invested in receiving love and approval from the relationship; therefore releasing yourself from the abusive relationship can also mean letting go of your search for the person's love, approval and indeed attention – regardless of how healthy or unhealthy it had been for you – it can feel excruciating.

In therapy I've noticed that one of the main barriers to healing from strained, toxic and abusive family relationships is worrying about if you've remembered or understood events accurately and if you have any right to label something as healthy or unhealthy. Our perception is often skewed and changes over time and in fact, when a client is telling me about their experience of strained, toxic or abusive family relationships, I wholeheartedly reserve judgement and any opinion on whether what they report is accurate. The complex emotions that engulf some families mean that how one person is received may be totally different to what they thought they were portraying.

An example: a parent may be intent on always telling the truth and see that as a healthy communication style, but their teenage son or daughter may receive their truthfulness as insulting, critical and even damaging, this is amplified if the parent themselves was parented through criticism and neglect as there is carried emotion being passed down a generation. It can be toxic to the teenager, leaving them with negative feelings about themselves and they may take on what we call introjections from their parent about who they are and what their parent thinks of them. These are usually more to do with what the parent thinks of themselves as a result of the parenting they experienced, and the parent isn't taking responsibility for their own lack of self-esteem and self-worth, so instead projects it onto their children. These interjections are classed as toxic because they can be carried around for decades and contribute to unhelpful self-talk and harm to the child's IWM, i.e. their relationship with themselves. Within this dynamic we have two very distinctive realities, and neither is necessarily wrong, but they are very different, and the result is something that is toxic to at least one person in the relationship.

Identifying Abuse

The majority of us find it hard to point out a family member's behaviour and call it abuse, even if we have an awareness that what is happening or has happened is unhealthy or dysfunctional. It's a difficult word to digest when you use it in relation to your reality and your family. There are a number of reasons for this but I think the most typical are:

1) Admitting we are on the receiving end of abuse can be painful, shameful and demoralising, particularly if it's been going on for a long time;

2) It can feel as if we are accusing someone of something and causing conflict; and

3) A process known as '*Groupthink*' is in action, which means that the unhealthy family system has put a lot of energy into sweeping things under the rug. Naming the abuse can feel like you are undermining the effort the family has put into how others perceive them and therefore feels like – and quite possibly is – a huge risk in terms of feeling and being accepted and loved in your family system.

Types of abuse	Expressions of abuse
Physical	hitting, punching, touching someone's body without consent
Psychological	criticising, gaslighting, verbally bullying, shouting, judging
Sexual	any sexual or sexualised touch without consent
Financial	controlling someone else's money, withholding money, using money as a bribe
Religious	using religious beliefs to control someone else's behaviour
Educational	denying someone the opportunity to receive an education

Chapter Three: FAMILY RELATIONSHIPS

Trauma Bonds

Moving past difficult relationships can feel like a momentous task because, at the risk of repeating myself, stemming from infancy, we are most invested in holding onto the belief that our family members love us and have always had our best interests at heart. At its most extreme, the specific reaction of continuing to protect and advocate for a family member who is toxic or abusive towards us often gets referred to as 'Stockholm Syndrome'. In more colloquial expressions we use the term *trauma bond*.

In her book *Why Love Matters*, psychotherapist Sue Gerhardt discusses the reasons why so many adults find it difficult to recover from traumatic experiences. The roots lie in babyhood, our connections to our caregivers and the stress we experience in early life. If we are trauma bonded through infant stress, we will almost certainly suffer from *relational Post-Traumatic Stress Disorder (PTSD)*. The PTSD born out of relational trauma is what Murray Bowens (see p. 49) and Pia Mellody's (pp. 49-50, 79-80) models seek to heal.

Trauma bonds can develop at any point in life, however, if you have experienced a repeated cycle of abuse or trauma alongside someone else – for example, siblings witnessing each other's abuse or the injury or death of a family member.

In terms of freeing yourself from trauma bonds, it's a process that involves identifying the trauma (pp. 54-8), getting yourself out of the relationship if you can (by creating and maintaining boundaries (pp. 39-42), handing back carried toxic emotions (pp. 70-71) and then undertaking the inner child healing work (p. 79).

Most of us need professional support to complete this process, although of course, if you feel capable, you can apply this list of things, at your own pace. If you suspect you may be trauma bonded to someone and you do not feel safe enough to break the bond alone, please seek further support and guidance (pp. 226-7).

People Pleasing

If we experience trauma bonds as a result of strained, toxic or abusive relationships in childhood, we can start to caretake our parents very early on through behaviours known as people pleasing and compulsive helping, believing that how our caregivers feel is our responsibility. This sense of responsibility is usually a result of the parent not having the knowledge or emotional regulation skills to be accountable for their own feelings.

If you've maintained your relationship with a toxic family member, trauma bonded or not, you will have needed to come up with all sorts of ways to justify their behaviour and tell yourself that one day you'll be able to do something that earns their love and approval. **Put simply, people pleasing is born out of the fear of losing love and approval.** Sometimes that might even mean making yourself responsible for the negative impact of their behaviour.

It's easy to dismiss people pleasing as something that we do to be nice to others and the most common myth is that people who compulsively please others are doing so because they want to be liked. I suppose there is some truth in that, but the deeper truth is that people-pleasing behaviour is an attempt to fill a fearful space deep inside that has been left by dysfunctional caregiving. It is sometimes argued that people pleasing is a PTSD response in itself. It is also a defence against conflict and allows you to side-step responsibility for your own thoughts, feelings and behaviours as you're busy trying to predict and control others. And the truth is, lots of us do it.

When you are active in your people pleasing you might feel that you're accomplishing something – but in an immature way. I use the word 'immature' in its true sense: a feeling of being younger, smaller and more vulnerable than you actually are, because the wounding that causes people pleasing behaviours have usually happened quite early in life.

The most common form of psychological toxicity that contributes to the development of pathological people pleasing is enmeshment and conditional love: 'I love and approve of you as long as you think the same as me/always meet my needs/never do or say anything I don't like', and so on. Parents may use phrases such as 'I love you, but I don't like you right now' or they may accuse an offspring of disliking *them* – these types of words can instil levels of fear in children of any age, but the younger we are, the more serious and threatening they seem to our survival. These messages can lead to what should be an unnecessary need to regain a sense of love and approval from the caregiver. If we take this one step further, 'I am not likeable/lovable' can become a negative core belief that is then taken into relationships outside the family and can turn into a desperation to be liked and loved, resulting in a compulsive need to please others in adulthood.

Compulsive Helping
Compulsive helping is another unhealthy behaviour that often slips under the radar. It comes in two forms: submissive and dominant. It is a specific part of co-dependent behaviour that means, in either a passive or prevailing way, you'll be taking liability for things that are someone else's responsibility in order to gain approval because your self-worth is dependent on what other people think of you.

An interesting thesis written in 2022 by Katy. L. Workman focused on the development of helping behaviours in late adolescence (a time of pattern establishing behaviours for adult life). The thesis found that although compulsive helping is positively correlated with pro-social behaviours, people who feel compelled to help others are far more likely to ignore personal signals that things have gone too far even when the behaviour becomes personally disruptive or harmful. They also found that compulsive helping is related to higher levels of anxiety and the higher the anxiety the more likely the study participants were to engage in more helping behaviours that were personally harmful to themselves, in an attempt to relieve themselves from the anxiety they experienced (see Further Reading).

Submissive compulsive helping is active when you take on other people's responsibilities without their awareness. It is sometimes grouped into the rescuer/enabler role (pp. 144-7). For example, noticing a family member hasn't completed their chores and doing it for them without talking to them about it. The unconscious drive may be that you are trying to avoid the negative emotional consequences of your own and other peoples undesirable emotional responses – for example a parent expressing displeasure or getting angry.

Dominant compulsive helping is active when you're actively and noticeably trying to fix and rescue others therefore not permitting them to experience the consequences of their own behaviours, also sometimes grouped into the enabler/rescuer role (pp. 144-7), especially when they haven't asked for your help. For example stepping in to resolve an argument without being invited. The negative impact is that the people having the argument don't get to resolve what's happening between them, instead they could become reliant on you to make the difficult feelings go away.

Both people pleasing and compulsive helping are behaviours that help us believe that we have some control over how others feel towards us. It can take a long time to let go of your people pleasing and compulsive helping within your family and beyond, because we also have to come to terms with the fact that we cannot control others. We have to recover from the false belief that we have any sense of power and responsibility of how other people feel.

Exercise: Releasing yourself from a dysfunctional family system

Is there someone (or more than one person) that came to mind as you read this section? Bring that person/people to your mind's eye. Please remember that we are not about to blame or shame them; this exercise is about you taking the appropriate amount of responsibility for the relationship and starting to let go of familiar behaviours that no longer serve you by finding the root cause. Ask yourself the following questions:

1. *How do you feel when you are in the presence of this person? For example: do you feel unsafe, small, ashamed, angry, hurt, etc.?*
2. *How do you feel when you are alone after spending time with this person? For example: do you feel rattled, confused, shamed, hurt, misunderstood, unheard, angry etc.?*
3. *When was the first time you felt this way around this family member? For example: as a child, around seven years old, or as an adult, 25 years old.*
4. *Using the age you just identified, was there a significant event that changed things? Or are/were your feelings attached to a*

> specific behaviour or trait that you observed? For example: 'My parents got divorced when I was seven, that's when I started to feel this way' or, 'I always felt that way, but I thought it was normal until I was old enough to realise differently.'
> 5. Can you identify any people pleasing or compulsive helping behaviours that have made their way into adulthood with you?
> 6. Would you like to change any of them?
>
> The way you answer the final two questions here tells us what we need to know. If there was a significant event, like a divorce, a death, or any other major change, then your work may be more about how you feel about the event, how that affected you, what you are carrying for others and the resulting behaviours you've developed to cope with what happened. If you identify that you've always felt that way, then you need to look more closely at the family dynamic and transgenerational trauma that is still impacting you negatively.

MOVING ON

As we mature, we start to take better care of ourselves and depend on our primary caregivers less and less, while we learn that our own way of taking care of ourselves is dependable. The dependence we once had on our family members becomes ***interdependence***. And then, at some point in our adult lives, if our relationships with ourselves is healthy, most of us realise we are actually better at looking after ourselves than our caregivers were or indeed are.

By this point we are no longer enmeshed and we are able to exercise autonomous and independent views as well as attitudes about our life and the world around us without feeling worried about negative consequences. This is frequently a difficult transition for both caregiver and child (of any age), as it involves letting go of the belief that we need love and approval from our caregiver to survive. The parent needs to step aside to allow their adult child to practise looking after themselves. This can bring up a range of difficulties for all involved and we will now take a look at three of them: *separation anxiety*, *conflict* and *grief*.

Separation Anxiety

One reason that people return to enmeshed, toxic or even abusive relationships is that they don't feel they can cope with the set of emotions that separation evokes.

If, due to a dysfunctional family system, we know no way to work through these difficult emotions, other than returning to the strained, toxic or abusive relationship, then that is what we'll do. When we do this we also forfeit the opportunity to build on our ability to emotionally regulate ourselves and separate in a healthy way which can hinder us in relationships as adults outside our family too.

Our denial systems play an especially clever part when it comes to separation: they allow us to effectively unsee anything that might be considered toxic or abusive in order not to have to separate and maintain our survival within the family. This usually comes out in therapy when someone says, 'I just thought that was normal…'. The experience of separating from what you thought was 'normal' can even feel life threatening. But holding onto denial can lead us into toxic friendships, as well as toxic romantic and sexual relationships as adults, because we carry the belief, stemming from the stress around separation, that if we are not loved and approved of, our basic needs will not be met and we might not survive separation in any form.

I am often enlightened about the different ways separation anxiety shows up in us as adults. Often, we don't call it separation anxiety. Instead, we say things like:

- 'My parents are always making decisions for me.'
- 'My siblings will disapprove of me if I do "X".'
- 'I could never tell my relation about "X".'
- 'I feel scared to tell my stepfather that I disagree with his view on "X".'
- 'I don't care about them anymore.'

And we may…
- Have difficulty leaving family situations or ending phone calls.
- Have difficulty staying connected in relation to family in the first place.
- Feel a sense of emotional obligation to a parent.

Chapter Three: FAMILY RELATIONSHIPS

- Base our decisions on what we think a family member would approve of rather than what we want to do.

To help you cope with separation from family members in a more efficient way, I'll first remind you of the inner child work we previously discussed. Yes, you may be anxious as an adult, but as your adult self, when your self-worth is intact, and you are using boundaries appropriately, you are totally capable of coping with separation, mainly because you know you can take care of yourself without the other person needing to guide you. It's the child inside who feels they will crumble when you start to individualise.

In order for your nervous system to trust that you will be able to tolerate the separation and look after yourself, the relationship between what practitioners call your 'functional adult' and your 'inner child' needs to be secure. You may be separating from a loved family member either for age-appropriate and developmental reasons, or because they are toxic or abusive towards you, and your inner child needs to know that the adult version of you is going to be there to look after them... always.

Exercise: Functional adult (adapted from the work of Pia Mellody)

After you have read this paragraph, close your eyes and take yourself to a time when you felt good about yourself. A time when you felt your self-esteem was in good shape and you had a good sense of your self-worth. A time you were able to create and maintain boundaries and you were behaving in ways that you are proud of.

If you can only find a time that matches one of these things, that is fine too. Take a really good look at the version of you that forms in your mind's eye. How old are you? What are you wearing? How do you feel? What is going on in your life at this moment in the past?

This image is your internal Functional Adult. This is the part of you that needs to be parenting your historic relational wounds and is going to develop a relationship with your internal inner child to support happier and healthier relationships with others.

> *Take this image of yourself and imagine it becoming part of your physical body so that you always have access to it. While working with clients using Pia Mellody's model (pp. 49-50, 79-80) I help them install this image into the upper right-hand quadrant of their torso – that's the space between the right shoulder and right hip. Some people like to imagine it as a puzzle piece clicking into place; others imagine the image of their Functional Adult shrinking down in size and stepping into their body – do what works for you.*

Coping with conflict

I've placed this piece about coping with conflict, and what happens when we disagree with our family, as the final section of this chapter, because you cannot authentically face conflict in a healthy way until you have at least some understanding of how you function in your family system. Coping with disagreements comes far more naturally when you come from a place of knowledge.

In addition, conflict often plays a part in our relationships as we develop a stronger sense of who we are as an adult (see the Functional Adult exercise above) and start to change and move on with our lives. For all the reasons already discussed, this can be particularly challenging, regardless of how healthy, unhealthy, toxic, abusive or happy your family relationships are.

Most therapists would argue that conflict is fundamental to healthy relationships. In fact, maybe it should even be the fourth item on the healthy family list (pp. 65-7). Conflict can be very helpful in aiding understanding, intimacy and boundaries. Additionally, most of the dysfunction we've covered could be boiled down to an avoidance of difference, conflict and disagreement as well as a fear of being rejected or abandoned by our family.

All of the items in the separation anxiety list are potential sources of conflict. They are often avoided because we don't know how to cope with the feelings involved, or address the issue and verbalise our reality, without feeling more anxious about being abandoned or rejected by someone who's supposed to care for us and love us.

There are, of course, families who are often in conflict. They don't feel scared of conflict, they fight and shout at each other a lot, but they do not use the conflict opportunity to get to know each other better; instead they use it to gather ammunition against each other for the next fight. For some families this is how they stay in relation to each other – as tense as it can be. If there is no healthy intimacy, conflict is, sometimes, the only way people know how to stay close to each other – and as strange as it may sound, it is still an attachment style. You might recognise your family here, or maybe your family is more of the conflict avoidant type, where you attempt to keep a lid on anger and unhappiness and zip your lip when conflict threatens itself.

Something to try out
As I explained at the start of this chapter, there isn't any one trick, secret or formula I can provide that will fix any particular rift. But if there is one thing I can offer, on top of you becoming more aware of your role in your family and how you want it to change, I would suggest active listening.

Active listening means that even when you disagree with something, whether it's political, something personal, or a specific behaviour someone is engaging in, you listen to their point of view. It's harder than it sounds, especially with family members because there is so much history to contend with. And very often we listen to react and fight our corner rather than listen to understand and respond. There is a word for this: ***diaphobia*** – the fear of being influenced by others, and it is probably most noticeable when we are in conflict. I first read about this in Phillipa Perry's *The book you wish your parents had read* (see Further Reading).

What I am about to suggest may sound very simple and if you've done any family therapy you may recognise it. In reality it takes a lot of effort and practice to employ as a life skill and indeed therapists literally train in active listening for years before they qualify.

The best way to practise active listening is to repeat back to the other person, EXACTLY, WORD FOR WORD, what you've heard without changing the tone, and allow them to correct you if you mis-repeat what they have said. Be aware that when you mis-repeat someone's words (and it is 'when', not 'if', because you will) they are likely to feel angry about it. It takes real skill to repeat verbatim what you've heard, rather than translate, interpret or omit things. So keep practising, and don't take responses personally.

Repeating, word for word, what the other person says achieves three things:

Firstly, it defuses any high emotional charge, because when we have evidence that someone is listening, we can let our defences drop, since we don't need to be further reinforcing our views and fighting to get our reality heard.

Secondly, it gives the other person an opportunity to hear what they've said and see if it still sounds true when repeated. It is important to note that sometimes when we repeat back what has been said and it doesn't come across favourably, the other person can take offence. If the other person maintains their own dysfunctional behaviours, you may find they attempt to manipulate the situation at this point. If this happens, calmly ask them to repeat what they said and try again. If they continue to feel offended and attack in response, my advice is to set a boundary and leave the situation, they may not be someone you can do this exercise with, but it's good that you found that out so you can keep yourself safe in the future.

Lastly, it gives you a chance to take a moment before you decide how to respond, which means you are less likely to withdraw your own reality or be on the attack.

In a nutshell, a lot of conflicts between family members are eased when all parties feel heard and *listened* to. You don't need to agree, you just need to hear the other person and show concern, interest and understanding towards their point of view. I would suggest you practise this with a safe family member (or friend/partner if no family member is available) as often as possible while you are not in conflict, so that when conflict arises you have the tools at your fingertips.

Having said all of that, disagreeing with a family member may continue to feel like an uncomfortable place to be. It usually is. But persist in this process: stick to your reality, work on your boundaries, allow yourself the gift of listening and being listened to – and, if it's appropriate, allow yourself to be influenced by the other person's views and opinions. You are going to have difficult feelings. Active listening doesn't that take away, it just creates emotional space so you can better communicate those feelings, should you wish to.

I hope this section has highlighted some useful information both theoretically and personally. As you work through the remaining sections in this book, I will refer back to family relationships, so don't fret if it feels like we haven't covered what you need or it feels like a lot to take on right now, the connections we make in the following chapters will help things come together more securely. Lastly, may I just ask you take a moment, knowing all you know now, to reflect on the question at the start of this chapter – *how would relationships be different for you if you'd had an entirely 'functional' family?*

Summary

1. *Your family of origin is your stencil to most other relationships. Understanding it makes understanding most other relationships easier.*
2. *The majority of us carry experiences for family members and this can cause resentment and fracture connections.*
3. *Healthy families respect each other and use boundaries out of love to create a sense of safety.*
4. *It's difficult to work on family relationships because we tend to fear being abandoned or rejected. This is called separation anxiety.*
5. *Conflict is helpful in building healthy intimacy if you are able to actively listen to each other and feel heard in your reality.*

Chapter Four:
FRIENDSHIPS

Reflective Question: 'When you were a child, was making friends easy or difficult?'

WHAT IS A FRIENDSHIP?

After our Family of Origin, the next set of relationships we build are friendships. This section will focus on building nourishing friendships and we'll use what you've previously read to help you let go of relational experiences that may have affected or still be affecting your friendships in ways you haven't chosen.

When I use the term relational experiences in a friendship context, I am referring to how patterns from your FOO, or negative experiences within historical friendships, affect your adult friendships in the here and now. This will once again involve you looking at the psychology of the relationship and your part in its dynamic, as well as the type of friendships you're attracting and choosing to keep.

While writing this book I read Elizabeth Day's book, *Friendaholic*. In one of her chapters she talks about the importance of your relationship with yourself and how it supports your choices around who you choose to be friends with. The more you understand about yourself, the more likely you are to choose people who will love you for being yourself. In addition she shares how friendships are vital because these are the people who accept us outside of our family roles, and therefore they allow us to access versions of ourselves we may never have known about otherwise. Day's approach is different to what we're doing here, because it's written from her own experience of using friendships to compensate for a lack of self-worth and she explains first-hand how she's improved the relational health of her friendships over time. A lot of it is backed up by research around friendships too. I won't be able to do it justice here (sor-

ry, Elizabeth) so I'd highly recommend it as Further Reading.
In this section, my fundamental message is that your self-worth need not rely on how many friends you have, or how much people like you, or don't like you. Friendships can indeed teach us about ourselves, but you also need to work on intrinsically befriending yourself before you'll be able to let others be able to earnestly do the same...

Defining what friendship is
Friendships come in all sorts of shapes and sizes depending on age, culture, values and more. It is beyond the scope of this book to cover friendships or any other type of relationship in every single form they may take. So instead, I do my best to explore the broadness of the topic and focus on your wellbeing within the types of friendships you choose to pursue and keep.

For clarity, throughout this chapter, when I use the word 'friend' I don't mean acquaintances or people you chat to at work – we'll cover those in the Workplace relationships chapter (see p. 162 Nor do I mean people you vaguely keep in contact with on social media – we'll get to those relationships in the Online chapter (see p. 187). When I use the word 'friend' I am referring to social relationships that have meaning and gravitas attached to them. Friends are the people who would leave an evident space were they not in your life.

Most research points to friendships being founded on common interests, a desire to avoid loneliness, sharing and reciprocation. If we break these aspects down further, we get to things like trust, fun, shared interests, a sense of humour, empathy, effort, love, support, good conversation and availability, all of which help create nourishing friendships. But there are also times when we allow friendships into our lives that are not made up of all these good things, either because of a low self-worth, or as a means of distracting ourselves from facing our own problems.

Even if you are not completing the exercises in written form, make a note for this next one, in the margins or at the back of the book, as we will be coming back to this list later. If you haven't got a pen right now, make the list on your phone.

Exercise: What makes up a friendship to you?

Brainstorm your personal definition of friendship. We'll come back to it at the end of this chapter to see if you want to add to it or change anything about it. Here are some questions to prompt your thinking:
- What draws you towards potential friends?
- Are there any common characteristics you can see in those you consider your friends?
- What do the people you call your friends add to your life?
- What would you miss the most if your friends were not around?

WHEN YOU WERE A CHILD, WAS MAKING FRIENDS EASY OR DIFFICULT?

The reflective question at the start of this chapter is an easy question to answer for most. I've noticed over the years that the majority of people in therapy can clearly recall their experience of making, or not making, friends as a child, even if they have few other memories. This is probably because, from an early age, friendships are important to us.

I've seen pretty much an even split between those who found making friends as a child easy and those who found it difficult. This is often indicative of a person's lifetime experiences of building and sustaining companionships mixed with their FOO hallmarks, plus their natural inclination towards introversion or extroversion, all of which we will cover in this chapter. Interestingly, it is often the eldest sibling or only children who are more likely to struggle with making friends, because they are not born into a situation where they need to accommodate a 'peer' – whereas a second- or third-born child has the experience of accommodating a peer from day one.

If I ask the same question about adulthood however, regardless of birth order, the majority of people tell me they find it hard to create new, meaningful, friendships and maintain both new and old friendships. I generally refraid from making major

Chapter Four: FRIENDSHIPS

gender generalisations, even though they talk about it less, but this is more common in adult men than it is for women.

Whichever camp you feel you fit into, it's important as you read on to remember that there is no judgement, no wrong or right and no good or bad. If you have lots of friends but worry about the quality of your friendships, we'll tackle that and if you are someone who would like more friends in your life, we'll look at how you can make that happen for yourself too.

Early Starts
Although I agree with Elizabeth Day's writings, as stated at the start of this chapter, that it is important to know yourself and choose friendships from a place of awareness, it doesn't start out like that. As children, we cannot and do not know ourselves well and we have much less of an internal focal point from which to choose healthy relationships. So, a bit like our family relationships, friendships can teach us things about who we are and how we function in relationships outside our FOO, but rarely do we get to truly choose who we befriend based on self-awareness until we are much older. So, let's look at the earliest seeds of friendship and how they grow...

As infants we seek out love, but we don't make friends as such. Yet, by the time we are a year old, we are developmentally capable of playing *alongside* our peers. Soon after that we start to demonstrate the social skills that connect us to others via playing *with* (rather than alongside) people of a similar age. As we become social creatures, we begin to develop what many would call 'friendships'. Often our early connections are based on who our parents or caregivers spend time with, or children we are in childcare with. These early connections are more about shared experiences, rather than things we hold in common.

As we get older, shared experiences and reciprocation become a more noticeable part of what connects us to people. Unless there is an underlying developmental issue, by the age of four, the majority of children seem to find ways of making friends and connecting with the people they are sharing experiences with, usually at nursery, school or during extracurricular activities. By the age of six, friendships have become important to us. It matters to us that our reality is believed and trusted and that we are safe with the people with whom we are building friendships.

This is the first time in our lives we have been exposed to a set of social cues outside our FOO and what they mean. This is a developmental milestone, where relationships start to matter to us totally independently of our caregivers and quite possibly, for the first time, we are taking the relational risk to invest in connecting with a non-family member. This milestone can also begin to change the way a child relates to themselves and others, as their experience is now influenced by more than just their FOO.

Up until around age seven, we rely exclusively on the caregivers and authority figures in our lives to support us in learning what is safe, what is not, and how to regulate our emotions. It's at around this age that we start to understand that there are different types of relationships available to us that can meet different needs and that we can co-regulate with people other than our family members.

Exercise: First friends

Can you remember who your first friend was? How old were you? What were the circumstances that brought you together? If you can't remember, what else comes to mind when I pose these questions?

On the interplay between caregivers and friendships

I'm slightly backtracking in terms of our timeline here, but I wanted to give you a good illustration of the interplay between the support we get from our family and how we behave socially. To demonstrate this I have chosen the concept of sharing here because, as mentioned earlier, sharing and reciprocation are two cornerstones of budding friendships. Now, we are not developmentally capable of genuinely sharing anything, whether that's our space, our toys, our feelings, or our caregivers, until we are at least three, probably four years old. Hence this is the age we can start to build actual friendships, rather than buddies we recognise and play alongside out of convenience.

Nonetheless, I've witnessed parents telling their two-year-olds off for 'not sharing'. The problem with this is that the child is being told off for simply being developmentally appropriate by the person who is best placed to teach them the social skill they're requiring. If the child, seeking approval from the caregiver, exhibits a 'fawn' response (see pp. 55-6) by willingly parting with whatever it is they are being told to 'share', under the belief that sharing is solely about giving without grasping the concept of reciprocation, it may lead the child to develop a perception (and an IWM) of being undeserving. As the child matures, a struggle with maintaining a sense of self-worth can manifest in difficulties around receiving not only material possessions but also emotional support within friendships and other relationships. The developing negative core belief that we are undeserving can gather steam, and the really sticky part comes in when the same caregiver calls them a 'pushover' or a 'people pleaser' and starts advising them to assert themselves. How confusing must this be for a young child who is biologically driven to please others in order to secure love!?

In an ideal world, the parent, caregiver or authority figure would teach and pass on a sense of empathy and tolerance, these being the fundamental traits that drive being able to give and receive authentically. From my own experience I've noticed that, for now, my toddler seems to grasp the concept of taking turns instead of sharing. She understands that if she waits a little longer, she may get a turn with whatever it is she is wanting to do and that someone else having a turn doesn't mean anything has been taken away from her. If she is playing with something and someone else wants a turn, she is also within her right to say no, but usually a few minutes later she is done and content for someone else to have a go. The message needs to be that you don't have to give anything away if you don't want to right now. This helps the child to learn their worth and navigate reciprocation appropriately within friendships, reducing the likelihood of their 'fawn' response developing into chronic people pleasing and supporting a sense of inherent self worth.

Exercise: People Pleasing Check-In

This exercise is about checking in on any people-pleasing behaviours that you might carry into your adult friendships.

For the rest of this week, each time a friend asks you to do something, instead of saying 'yes' or 'no', try saying 'Let me get back to you' (even if you're sure you know what your final answer will be). You can try this with anyone in your life, not just your friends!

Take the time you've carved out for yourself by using these statements to process and consider:

a. What you REALLY want to do
b. How you REALLY feel about it
c. Where you are responding from. For example, is your response coming from a childlike place that is seeking love and approval via pleasing others?

As you move away from people-pleasing behaviours in friendships, you might feel a sense of guilt. The guilt comes from a developmental phase that should have been allowed to occur within your FOO when you were little. Guilt and fear often arise from separation anxiety and the worry associated with not receiving approval from caregivers, now being transferred on to friendships.

What happens in friendships when our attachment style tends to be insecure?

Beyond our primary school years, as a matter of social survival, we are programmed to build friendships with people who can act as our allies. We need people on our team, and we are usually drawn to those we feel safe and calm around. But what happens if we are not familiar with safe and calm? Or we have been taught to people please or compulsively help others in order to feel included and liked? What kind of friends do we choose then?

Let me take you back to the monkey experiment in the Attachment section of this book (pp. 44-5). The baby monkeys who were not given a chance to create a secure attachment with a caregiver, when placed in peer groups of other monkeys, did not know how to socialise well at all. They struggled to interact with their peers of a similar age, leaving them as outsiders and without allies or friendships.

One of the major disrupters to developing healthy friendships before, as well as into, adulthood is an anxious, avoidant or disorganised attachment model. A strained, toxic or abusive home, or a lack of opportunity in practising socialising outside our FOO, for example being less able-bodied or those who were of school age during the pandemic, would also make it harder for us to gain the social awareness we need to choose healthy friendships. Some might simply not form attachments, or attach to people who seem familiar, replicating a negligent or abusive experience at home. Some may also repeat the neglect or abuse they were on the receiving end of with their peers, as they haven't been shown another way to treat people.

If you are anxiously attached you may play this out with friends from a young age. Attachment anxiety in friendships can show up as a concern about what other people think of you, a need to be reassured that your friend still likes you, and feeling possessive over friends. You might experience envy, resentment and jealousy within the relationship. Some children are pulled out of school due to what gets labelled as social anxiety, and of course that is a reality for some, but I am certain there are others who have not had a secure attachment experience at home, and therefore experience overwhelming anxiety when it comes to making friends: it is near impossible for them to be in social groups and find their allies.

Having said all that, the sad truth is that these days we get far less opportunity to practise social interactions. The connectivity we all have through smartphones and time spent online has totally changed what it means to create authentic allies, practise boundaries and build our self-esteem within friendships. It's very easy to hide behind a screen and avoid full responsibility for our impact on others and therefore we're prompted less often to consider our attachment responses within friendships.

HOW WE CHOOSE OUR FRIENDS

At the start of this chapter, I gave you an exercise to prompt your thinking about what qualities you seek out in your friendships. Most of us can make this list retrospectively. We rarely have a list of qualities that we tick off before we decide to be friends with someone. Less consciously however, a part of us is always seeking out something specific.

As we get older, throughout secondary school and into early adulthood, we usually develop an awareness of how we show up in friendships, and we become more socially adept. We get the hang of sharing and reciprocation in line with our self-worth and our attachment styles may even change, depending on the experiences we go through. We learn about empathy and tolerance and start to recognise the type of person we'd choose to spend time with, and the type of person we don't get on with so well.

The people you choose to keep around are likely to be those you feel know how to be in a friendship with you, either because you've been sharing space and experiences for an extended period of time, creating an encyclopaedia of memories that assist you in sustaining those connections later in life, or the friend seems to fulfil the things you look for in the company you keep. You may also have dynamics and roles you play with each other which show up more clearly the more familiar you become. These roles may mirror the roles you play in your family, or they may allow you to explore new ways of behaving which are not available to you within your FOO.

The dynamics which attract us to each other, and therefore the friends we choose, are not the most conscious of processes so you could argue that, especially while we are younger, we do not 'choose' the people we gravitate towards or the roles we play. Our choices are affected by what our caregivers taught us about relating to others through mirroring and ***modelling***, as well as our lived experiences of friendships, until the time and experience comes where we can more consciously choose friendships which are nourishing for us and/or seem worth investing in.

Regardless of the type of friendship, whether it is long or short lived, we tend to choose friends based on the roles we feel most comfortable in. Some people take on a maternal role, some people pride themselves on being the organiser, while others might go down in history as the party animal, the outsider or the studious one. Take some time now to reflect on a friendship group you are in or have been in and consider what role you have played and if it is the same or different to your family dynamics. Thinking about this may help you understand why you choose the friends you choose.

Reflecting on the roles you play in friendships and the impact they have on your choices will help you understand the purpose of the friendships you've created, for better or worse. For example, if your role was the maternal one you may be more likely to choose friends who you sense need looking after; on the flip side, if you feel you need looking after you'll be more attracted to people who give off maternal qualities. If you're the party animal, you'll most likely choose friends who will join in with your partying rather than challenge it (should it need challenging). In both these scenarios you may be exploring a new part of yourself or repeating a pattern you're already familiar with.

Adaptations

However, if our self-worth isn't intact, we can find ways of fulfilling a social role (like the ones listed above) that gains us a sense of belonging and approval for being something that is inauthentic to us. For example, realising that being attractive can increase your popularity often moves people to focus on their appearance, which can gain them social approval, rather than nourishing connections based on authentic connections between personalities. Same applies for being the 'cool' one, the clever one, the busy one etc. We change ourselves to feel like we fit in rather than achieving the sense of genuine belonging we crave. And if we do this often enough we can feel as if we lose sight of who we actually are, often expressed in therapy when someone says 'I don't know who I am anymore'.

This whole process requires people to choose us, rather than us choosing them, so we hold on to the role that works to get away from our relationship with ourselves and compensates for not feeling good enough, or for feeling that we are too much for others to handle (both categorised as self-worth issues). We essentially create an adaptation of ourselves which ensures a level of social survival and can also mean we are not connecting with others from an authentic place.

Adaptations usually work well for a period of time but because they disconnect us from our authenticity in relationships with ourselves and others, over time we often end up feeling lonely, unseen, misunderstood and isolated within a friendship group.

For me, understanding why I chose the people I chose to be friends with, adapted or authentic, and what it was I was seeking, has led me to a place of knowledge and empathy. It can be painful and also eye-opening to unravel the hard truths about the things you do to secure friendships and the choices you make, but when you do the healing work around it you have the chance to create far more authentic friendships going forward with people who know who you really are rather than the adaptations born out of a place of low self-worth.

Maintaining the friendships you've chosen (or not)

Choosing which friendships you want to maintain is one of the cornerstones of adulthood. But not all of us are active in this choice. Rarely are we psychologically prepared for the change in our friendships that occurs when we are no longer automatically in each other's presence several times a week – for example, when we finish attending school, college or university – and we have to invest more time and energy in choosing to stay in each other's lives. Emotional distance can grow, particularly if our investments have been in people who we try to connect with through adaptations of ourselves rather than via our authenticity.

If you're like me, you may have maintained approximately zero friendships from your school days. I moved school quite often and sometimes I put my lack of long-term childhood friendships down to that, but the truth is I can only really guess at why none of my relationships sustained the test of time. I suspect it's because I didn't actively choose to maintain them or I had other priorities. I am also an eldest child, and was an only child for a full five years before my sister came along, so maybe making friends and holding on to them is just not something that came very naturally to me.

I suspect my mental health had a lot to do with it. It declined while I was a teenager, and as I moved into my adult years my eating disorder became more important to me than any relationship. Ironically, I believe a large contributor to me losing control over my eating and not eating was the ***power dynamics*** I was exposed to at school (see p. 50), and not knowing how to choose and connect with people who would ally with me as I was, authentically. The school environment I experienced, that was supposed to provide an opportunity to build friendships and teach me social skills, did exactly the opposite. It taught me that I would be shamed and rejected, not just by one person or one friendship group, but by an entire school of people.

Reflecting on this now, I can see how my unconscious expectation that I would be rejected by my peers prevented me from genuinely settling in any other peer-driven spaces, and on some level, I unconsciously chose not to maintain friendships as a result.

I often find myself feeling sad about not having a larger friendship circle and I regret that I don't have people who've known me through the years, through thick and thin, for better or worse, people who know my full story so to speak. But I was simply so involved with my own problems that my ability to give and receive friendship was totally thwarted. I think, if I could change one thing about my life experience, this would be it.

So, what could I have done differently that would have maintained more of my friendships? What could have given me a different result?
1. I could have been more honest with my friends.
2. I could have let more people in when they showed care and concern towards me.
3. I could have carried less shame about who I was into my friendships.
4. I could have known how to be more interested and empathetic towards others.
5. I could have isolated myself less.

I encourage you to make your own list of things that, on reflection, if you had known, you could have done differently. It doesn't need to look anything like mine but it'll help you know how you want to behave in the future if you find new friendships you'd like to maintain.

The purpose of the list is not to shame ourselves, it's to strengthen the maintenance points in your current day friendships. It helps acknowledge and empower changes we wish to make without giving yourself a hard time because the behaviours that have negatively impacted your friendships are, more often than not, simply a repetition of unhealed relational wounds.

Frenemies

Frenemies are friends you choose to keep close even though there is a borderline unhealthy rivalry or dislike for each other. I am sure I am not the only one who has spent time wondering why I am maintaining a friendship despite struggling to protect myself and feeling bad about myself within it. These types of friendships can even cross the line into what could be considered bullying. They are often full of sarcasm, slightly over-the-mark teasing, and lack support and reciprocation.

When I refer to bullying here, either in the overt or covert sense, what I mean is calculated cruelty from one person towards another where hurt is intentional either through action or inaction. It has to be said, not all frenemies are bullies, but if you have been bullied or indeed have been in another type of abusive relationship, you'll have learned to put up with a frenemy that teases, criticises and punishes you more than someone who hasn't previously been a victim of bullying or abuse. You may even choose people like this because it feels familiar to you.

You're more likely to put up with it because your sense of self-worth has been damaged through your previous experiences and you believe that you are not worth more within your friendships. On the other side of things, if you were the bully, you may now feel a sense of shame about how you behaved, unless you are still bullying people in adulthood – in which case you will likely still deny that you are a bully in order to justify the behaviour, and use more covert tactics to feel powerful which may indeed move you into the frenemy category.

The interesting thing is that all these people – frenemies, bul-

Chapter Four: FRIENDSHIPS

lies, victims – actually have a similar sense of shame driving their behaviours. They are often outsiders who struggle to know where their place is in a group. There might be something going on at home that contributes towards the tendency to get caught up in punishing dynamics and this unconscious process drives a person to either act out through attacking others, or act in by withdrawing and potentially also attacking themselves. See my adapted 'compass of shame' diagram below.

This diagram was originally developed by Dr Donald Nathanson in 1992. According to Dr Nathanson, shame is an important regulator of social behaviour. It is triggered when experience of positive emotions like joy, excitement or pleasure gets interrupted. This is important when it comes to frenemies because, when sharing something positive with a frenemy, the response usually dampens and ruins the experience sending the other person into shame. Likewise with bullies, although you're less likely to be sharing your news with them, you might be walking through the office minding your own business, feeling fine and then receive an email, hear a snigger or a comment which interrupts your current state and triggers shame within you. See Further Reading if you're interested in Nathanson's work.

When I explain it like this, maybe you can see how the people who engage in these types of connections are all a bit lost in terms of their place in a friendship group, and so they adopt these extreme adaptations to compensate.

You're probably right if you're reflecting on a bully or a frenemy and struggling to piece together what I've said because they appear to feel no shame and didn't seem to care what their impact on others was. I can explain... shame is such an awful emotion for humans to experience that some people literally cannot contain it and they have to get rid of it by passing it on to other people (see info on carried emotion on pp. 56-7). Think about it like this – most of what other people do and say has very little to do with you, and everything to do with them. When someone belittles someone else they are projecting their feelings of shame and low self-worth onto a person whose vulnerabilities reflect their own because they just cannot cope with having that part of themselves reflected back to them. Indeed, with a frenemy, their envy gets the best of them – they attempt to destroy the parts of themselves they see in others through criticism and *envious attacks*.

MAKING AND MAINTAINING HEALTHY FRIENDSHIPS AS AN ADULT

Friendships as an adult are not the passive experiences they are when we were children, since we are no longer in positions where we are forced to bond with a random selection of people. Now we get to choose who we hang about with and do not need to stand for complicated power dynamics if we don't want to. Friendships now require self-awareness, attention towards the things that matter, and ongoing care if they are going to survive.

If we are not socialising or indeed not socialising with the right people, we feel low, anxious and depressed. There is research from 2020 to support the hypothesis that having close friendships acts as a preventive measure against depressive feelings (see the Psychiatry Online link in the Further Reading section if you want to know more about this).

Maybe, also, when we go off and build our adult lives, the time spent apart makes it feel like there's too much to catch up on, or maybe we've all just changed and grown too far apart in different directions. I'm speculating about this because, like lots of people, when my own self-esteem is low, my critical internal voice will tell me that I don't have any friends and it's because people don't like me or are not interested in me anymore. Even more so since I became a mum, I've found the change in my friendships difficult to manage, and feel less and less connected to a community, and have less and less energy and time to put into maintaining friendships. It's true that the parenting thing really does change you and your priorities have no choice but to reorder themselves, but even with my friends who have also started having kids, or indeed mum friends that I've met, I find it hard to maintain connection at times.

Based on what I know about the psychology of friendships, this difficulty has actually got nothing to do with my worth or how likeable I am. As I discussed above, friendships are most often created through shared experiences, and the main problem is that despite the shared experiences in our histories, there is not enough sharing happening in our adulthood to entice a nourishing friendship. And that is why, at least in my experience, it can feel harder to make and maintain friends as adults. This is of course not true for everyone – some people manage to continue to have shared experiences with long-term friends for the majority of their life. We may be able to justify the differences between those who do and those who don't by looking at Social Arousal Levels.

Social Arousal Levels

Social arousal levels are helpful to know about with regards to making and maintaining adult friendships because they help us understand our optimal levels of motivation (in this case directly related to friendships but relevant across all parts of life). They are related to how and why we choose things (in this example, friendships), the way we do things, and how we maintain a sense of psychological and social balance, known more academically as social *homeostasis* – a term created by Walter Bradford Canon who also came up with the 'fight, flight, freeze, fawn' stress response theory (see pp. 55-6), while we do things.

Interestingly, our social arousal needs are determined by how we feel we recharge best and find homeostasis, rather than how much time we spend actually socialising. For example, if you recharge best alone, you'll be on the more introverted end of the spectrum, whereas if you recharge more effectively around other people, you're on the more extroverted end of the spectrum. There is also a middle ground – the ambivert; you're an ambivert if the way you recharge varies from day to day.

The other indicator is how you process things. If you tend to process stuff out loud and need to talk through what's going on in your mind with someone in order to make sense of it, you'd be placed towards extroversion. On the other hand, if you are someone who processes things quietly – for example, you have to think about things before you discuss them with someone else – you'll be more introverted. If you're an ambivert, this will change on a day-to-day basis as well as, potentially, over the space of a week or month.

As with most of these personality theories, it's a spectrum. You do not have to fit yourself into one box or another. Over the course of your lifetime you may experience all three social arousal types and find you need to make changes in how often you are around your friends compared to how often you are alone – depending on the most effective way for you to achieve a feeling of homeostasis (balance). The important thing is to be aware of how this affects the quality of the friendships you want to build, and to be able to communicate any changes you're noticing in order to maintain your friendships.

Personally, I'd put myself on the more introverted end of the spectrum. I say this not because I have a small group of friends or because I am shy. I am not very shy at all. I'm pretty confident and not easily socially flustered or embarrassed, but I am 'A Highly Sensitive Person' (see Further Reading) which means I feel a lot, often, and I need time to observe before I get involved, which people have mistaken for shyness, most of my life. I'd say my social arousal levels are mostly affected by my overall wellbeing, my sense of responsibility in life, how much sleep I am getting and also my mental health, so it's a mix of my nature and my current life experience.

Shyness and introversion do not go hand in hand. Shyness is a painful place to be, and it is a family member of shame. It's very hard to make friends when you're in your shyness. Introversion and being highly sensitive are entirely different to being shy. You do not have to change your introversion or sensitivity in order to build friendships, you just need to know how to navigate it to get what you need. However, if you do identify as shy, you may choose to work on the root cause of your shyness to make relationships feel a bit less painful. You can do this by actively working on your self-esteem and boundaries in friendships, as well as checking out the 'Social Events Workout' section in my first book, *Your Mental Health Workout* (see Further Reading list).

Similarly, extroverts are not always outgoing and confident, although they do feel the need to socialise more and may have a larger friendship group because that is where they refuel, so to speak. Some of the most extroverted people I know actually have a strong sense of self-doubt, which might in turn essentially mean they feel more shy than someone who is introverted. Extroverts, however can usually maintain more friendships than someone who is introverted, but they also struggle to know where the quality friendships are.

So, I suppose what I am saying here is: do not judge anyone by their introversion or extroversion. All is not always what it seems and being mindful about your own social arousal levels can help you find balance and get the needs you require to be met within your friendship.

Exercise: Social Arousal Levels

Would you classify yourself as an introvert, ambivert or extrovert? Think about how you recharge and how you process information. Give specific examples as to why you have answered the way you have. What other factors affect your social arousal levels?

How many friends do we need?

Research from the 1990s by Robin Dunbar, a professor of evolutionary psychology at Oxford University, indicates that regardless of our social arounsal levels, as adults, we only <u>need</u> three to five close relationships to feel fulfilled, and they don't have to all be friends. Our inner circle will most likely include a romantic partner, if you choose to have one, and/or a family member. So really we need very few close friends. Even more importantly, the research shows that if we have too many friendships on the go, we become more vulnerable to feeling overwhelmed and we find it much harder to maintain the quality and structure of each one.

The magic number of maximum relationships that a human can accommodate is 150, known as Dunbar's Number. Over 150, we simply do not have the cognitive ability to maintain the relationship with any form or depth. There are studies that have deconstructed Dunbar's Number theory and come up with vastly different numbers, of anything between 2 and 520 people. However, from all I've read I would confidently say that Dunbar's number is well supported.

And... please, don't freak out about the number 150 – you do not need to maintain 150 friendships. I certainly do not have 150 friendships or even relationships that I am actively maintaining. Dunbar's Number works in layers (see diagram opposite). Up to 100 of the relationships you maintain could be people you simply stay in contact with tenuously, for example on social media, the other 50 will be a mix of close friends, good friends, colleagues and family members. Have a look at the exercise below and see who fits into which layer.

Exercise: Dunbar's Number

Have a look at the example diagram. Imagine yourself at the centre and think about who you feel would fit into each layer of your life.

Chapter Four: FRIENDSHIPS

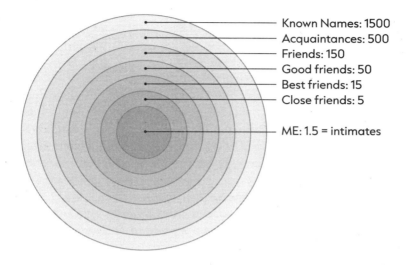

Known Names: 1500
Acquaintances: 500
Friends: 150
Good friends: 50
Best friends: 15
Close friends: 5
ME: 1.5 = intimates

Another theory I really like that supports this thinking is Socioemotional Selectivity Theory (SST). Developed by psychologist Laura Carstensen, SST aims to explain your social motivation over your lifespan. The idea is that with age, people become more selective and prefer to invest time and energy into more meaningful people and activities. SST supports the theory that having fewer friends minimises the emotional risks associated with relationships, and that reducing your social network to only those who can satisfy your emotional needs provides all the psychological support and emotional regulation we need.

There are many other reasons we shrink or grow our social circles. For example, when we move cities, countries, continents; when our career takes precedence in our lives; when we are made redundant; when our mental or physical health is not at its finest, or indeed when it improves as we may make major social changes. Also, when we meet a new romantic partner; when we go through a break-up with a romantic partner; when we get married; when we become parents; when we don't become parents; when we get sick or injured. All of these things will no doubt impact the number of friendships you need to feel fulfilled.

In addition, sometimes, something in a person's history has led them to where they are in terms of the quality and quantity of friendships. Maybe they were cut out of a friendship group previously. Maybe they were, at one point, the most popular person in their circle, without being anything other than themselves, but as they grew older, dynamics and people changed, and they were left feeling that being themselves wasn't enough anymore. So, as an adult they carry a sense of not being good enough and of being a failure that wasn't around when they were a child. Hence, they may have fewer friends now than ever before, which may or may not work for them.

What I am trying to communicate is that, sometimes, we choose to shrink or grow our social circles from a healthy, thought-out place, and sometimes we do it from a place of fear and damaged self-worth. But let it be said that you need as many friendships as you feel you can maintain at that time. That may mean you need to let go of a friend here and there and at times seek out new friends.

The majority of the friendships you invest in should be able to meet your social needs and provide you with all the things a friendship ought to offer: care, support, trust reciprocation, common interests, good conversation, and anything else you'd add to your definition of friendship. Refer back to the start of this section and the defining friendship exercise on p. 116 as a reminder. The maintenance of your friendships shouldn't require any inauthentic adaptations of yourself.

INTIMACY IN FRIENDSHIPS

It's really easy to prioritise getting the quality intimacy we seek from romantic relationships over friendships, as if, somehow, romance is most important in life. I once even read that most adult friendships are just people bouncing off each other and debriefing about romantic partners – as if friends are just around to be shock absorbers for romantic relationships. What would happen if we worked as hard on processing and understanding our friendships and talked as much about them as we did our love lives? Our friendships would, quite possibly, gain more depth. We'd have a more common understanding of what friendship actually is and what is expected of us within a friendship and therefore more people would find themselves making healthier choices. But we don't, because unlike with romantic relationships, there is no verbal or non-verbal agreement about what friendship is. We don't lay down our hopes or expectations in friendships in the same way we do when we date someone. Yet lots of friendships will outlive your romantic encounters and they will be the relationships you turn to when you need comfort in the face of a broken heart. So maybe, quality intimacy with your friends is just as important as intimacy elsewhere.

One of the main things you can do to deepen the intimacy of a friendship is to be aware of how much time you are communicating within the relationship about yourself and hearing the other person in their reality, rather than gossiping or problem solving other relationships. I'd argue that spending your time talking about relationships other than the one right in front of you is an attempt to avoid intimacy within the friendship. *(I know, there was a time I'd raise my eyebrows at this statement too... stay with me.)*

If something feels difficult, and authentic intimacy within friendships is a difficult practice to maintain because it isn't the norm, many of us choose to give up. How many times have you wanted to cut a friend off rather than using your communication skills to clear the air because someone left you feeling angry or disappointed? It's far easier to block the intimacy by ignoring a friendship issue, cutting and running, or gossiping to or about others, than it is to face the big feelings and emotions that these bonds can trigger. If you keep cutting and running, you can end up very lonely, but it happens, sometimes unconsciously, without us realising.

The fact is, feeling our feelings is often inconvenient to us; as many of my clients have pointed out, there isn't time to always be feeling our emotions and expressing them in full force, particularly in relationships outside our family (of origin or creation). But there is a balance to be found, and it takes practice to accurately represent yourself and your emotions in an intimate way that builds quality friendships and feels comfortable to you.

How to build intimacy in friendships

So, let's get the glaringly obvious out of the way with regards to making and maintaining friends. If you find someone you want to spend more time with, you need to:

a. Connect with them on social media or exchange phone numbers
b. Contact each other
c. Arrange a time to meet up
d. Stick to the plan you've made
e. Repeat these steps

If you want to build more intimacy within your current friendships, you need to:

a. Be aware of how your FOO affects your behaviour in friendships
b. And what roles you tend to play in friendship dynamics
c. Have an awareness of your social arousal levels, which equate to you getting your wants and needs met in friendships
d. Be honest about your emotional wellbeing
e. Be prepared to tell the truth and be told the truth about feelings within the friendship
f. Be open to trust and being trusted

That said, when you apply these suggestions, what may surface are the less obvious aspects that might be affecting your ability to create intimate and reciprocal friendships as an adult.

Real or perceived unmet expectations, disappointments and resentments, as well as feeling abandoned or rejected by people you call or want to call your friends, can mean you retreat from friendships because of something happening in your internal world.

Below, I give more information about the less conscious drivers that can affect the intimacy of your friendships. This information will also apply in a different context when we talk about romantic relationships, and will probably relate back to your FOO too. Despite the context being different, your process around them is what is important.

Chapter Four: FRIENDSHIPS

Expectations

We all have expectations. They are usually based on our previous life experiences and on what amount and type of hope is in the mix (see pp. 11-14). For example, if your IWM tells you that people tend to like you and want to spend time with you then you will, generally speaking, expect that people you meet will like you and want to spend time with you. Likewise, if your life experience is that people don't seem to care about you then you will expect people not to care about you... and so on.

When we enter new social environments or experiences, our minds and bodies pick up a whole series of cues without our conscious awareness and we create predications based on these cues. Some would argue that this is how our emotions are created (see Further Reading: *How emotions are made*). That may be so, but it definitely is how our expectations are created.

Expectations are also formed when we have expectation put upon us, as we may well expect from others what was expected of us. For example, if in your family you were expected to play the scapegoat, when it comes to friendships you may carry this unhelpful pattern with you and either expect to be scapegoated, or expect there to be someone else to be the scapegoat.

You may also have completely healthy expectations for your friendships, like 'my friends will be loyal and reliable'. Again, these will likely come from your previous life lessons and be influenced by your IWM. Most of us find that our own personal set of expectations is made up of both healthy and unhealthy beliefs. Your work is to become conscious of both types and decide which expectations are realistic within your individual friendships.

Exercise: What are your expectations of friendships?

Think back to the work you did in the family chapter. What expectations did your family of origin create that you now carry forward into your friendships?

Disappointment

I vividly remember getting back into my car after my first therapy session as an adult and feeling a heavy sensation that turned out to be disappointment. I realised this feeling I was having, that was so familiar to me, was because, without my conscious awareness, I had set high expectations of what the therapy would be like, how the therapist would behave and even how the room would be set up, none of which had been met. It wasn't that the session wasn't helpful; it just didn't match with my expectations, and the sum of these things resulted in an experience of disappointment.

Being able to accurately identify the feeling of disappointment for the first time prompted an awareness that I'd been feeling and repressing disappointment in friendships for many years. I used to be the type of person who would change or make plans based on what I thought would please other people and gain me their approval. This meant I was living in an adaptation of who I was and wasn't putting my authentic self first, which meant my self-esteem was reliant on how others responded to me. My friendships held an unspoken expectation that people were not allowed to let me down because how I felt about myself was reliant on them showing and telling me I was worth their time and energy. Healthy people, in general, do not really like the feeling that they are responsible for upholding other people's self-esteem – it feels icky (as if personal space is being invaded) – and people will often back away from that dynamic. Even if they are not entirely sure why, they just feel uncomfortable.

Like many of the clients I've worked with on improving the quality of their friendships, I too found the feeling of being disappointed pretty unbearable. To cope, people often slip into dysfunctional behaviours that serve to numb the emotion. But once you know that feeling disappointed is a trigger for you, then you can choose to behave differently about it, if you want to.

Something I found useful and often pass on to others is always having a plan B. If Plan A was, let's say, to go to the cinema and for dinner with my friend, plan B would be something like this: still going to the cinema, either on my own – befriending myself with compassion and using it as an opportunity to build my relationship with the inner child in me that was feeling sad about being let down – or with someone else if they were free at the last minute. This strategy helped me cope with the horrible feeling of being disappointed, and facilitated a reframing of the disappointment experience as an opportunity to work on my relationship with myself.

Side note: I also used this strategy when I was on the dating scene. Having a plan of action if things don't go your way works in pretty much any relationship where you need to find a way of coping with potential disappointment.

Exercise: How have you coped with disappointment?

What unhelpful behaviours have you used to help you cope with feeling disappointed? For example: is there any kind of addiction or eating disorder present? Or maybe you've coped with feeling disappointed by using behaviours such as perfectionism, procrastination, intimacy blocking, or engaging with people who you know are toxic to you.

What alternative strategy could you use to help tolerate the feeling of disappointment?

Some options:

a. Have a plan B in mind.
b. Write a no-send letter/message to your friend. I'd suggest doing this in the notes app on your phone or as a voice memo NOT straight into your messaging app. The idea of a no-send message is that you get to process and give space to the emotions that are coming up without expecting a response from the other person. Read it back 48 hours later and see how you feel about it. You may choose to speak to your friend at that point. But don't send your no-send letter/message to them directly.
c. Reflect on what expectations led to you feeling disappointed and where those expectations come from (see previous exercise).

Abandonment

Generally, when we talk about feeling abandoned, we think about our childhoods and being abandoned by our caregivers. But as we get older and our Internal Working Model takes shape, we can start abandoning ourselves in response to others' behaviour. In my earlier example, when I was making plans based on what I thought others would want, I wasn't putting my own social needs first. Instead, I was abandoning myself, and so when my friends failed to show up, I'd be left disappointed and plummet into childhood emotions of pain, shame and abandonment.

The pain and shame that surfaces when we feel abandoned stems from the childhood belief that we are not good enough. So, here's something to consider: an adult cannot abandon another adult. If you are feeling abandoned by your friends, you are probably connecting to something unresolved in your childhood. You will need to work on not abandoning yourself. I did this via having my plan B and literally imagining my hurt inner child and taking them with me, using phrases such as: 'I'm sorry that your friend can't make it today. I can see you're sad about it, I'm sad too. Let's make sure we stay connected and have some fun together, we can always see your friend another time.'

Exercise: Working with abandonment pain

Consider how old (or young) you feel when you're in touch with abandonment pain. One way of figuring this out is to observe your body language. Have your shoulders hunched over? Are your arms crossed? How big or small do you feel? If you were to attach an age to your observations, what would it be? 4? 7? 10? 16? What was going on for you around that time that you might be reminded of now?

What phrases does the younger version of you need to hear?

NOTE: *The feelings will not vanish when you do this exercise. The goal is that, over time, you learn to cope more effectively and be more resilient in situations that used to leave you feeling abandoned.*

Chapter Four: FRIENDSHIPS

Rejection

As mentioned above, another adult **cannot** abandon you as an adult, but another adult **can** reject you. If you have been rejected by a friend or friendship group, you will know how painful it can be.

Being rejected can happen in a number of ways, whether it's being left out of a friendship group, being bullied or being cut off by a close friend. Perhaps you've been on the end of the silent treatment despite attempts to reach out – or perhaps you're the one who has done the rejecting and cut off friendships in the past.

Either way, the question that usually arises is: why?

Friends sometimes reject friends when they are finding something difficult or intolerable and they don't have the intimacy experience or skill set to explore a healthy way to work through it. Or they don't want to, for their own reasons. The thing about rejection and friendships is that we don't expect to be rejected by a friend because, unlike dating, there's no real agreement as to what the relationship is exactly. In contrast to romantic relationships where we are often consciously fearful of being rejected, when it happens within a friendship dynamic, it can take us by surprise.

Here's an example: A client I worked with was deeply hurt and felt rejected by a friend she had known for many years and really admired when her friend started declining invites to social events. My client was angry and responded by giving up on the friendship. A few years later my client found out the friend in question had died of breast cancer and that period of time where she was 'rejecting' my client was while she was deciding how to tackle her disease. Her rejection of invitations had nothing to do with how she felt towards my client. She was urgently creating space in her life for her final years.

This is why it is hard but helpful to practise not taking rejection personally. It always hurts but people reject people because they experience something outside of their window of tolerance, not necessarily in direct response to something you've said or done. You also have to be honest with yourself: if you've behaved in a way that you know may have warranted a friend rejecting you, then it's time to stop pretending you don't know why it's happening and maybe start a conversation with them, if you're prepared to be transparent and vulnerable enough to work through the conflict.

If you're the one doing the rejecting, make sure you understand why you are rejecting people who could be or continue to be your friends – particularly if you are reading this book with the goal of maintaining more of your friendships over time. If you are a rejector, you may start to notice that you feel the need to reject people at a particular point, maybe when the intimacy gets a bit too deep for you and when your fear of being seen for who you really are is activated. You might find this manifests, particularly in new adult friendships, demonstrated by you getting to a certain point and then deciding to stop bothering with what was a budding friendship. Or maybe you decide you don't like them after all. If so, can you spot a pattern?

Exercise: Free writing

Use the information above to do some free writing around your experience of being rejected or rejecting others. You don't need to come up with solid answers; just think of a time in your life that involved rejection and start writing. Notice what feelings come up as you do it and write them down. Do you feel anger? Sadness? Shame? Relief? This is an explorative exercise, so come back to it anytime you revisit rejection in your life and notice if anything has changed.

BUILDING STRONG FRIENDSHIPS – A RUNDOWN

Let's do a little rundown of all we've covered so far, so that you end this chapter with a very clear understanding of how friendships work for you and how to create and maintain them.

Ultimately, building strong friendships as an adult starts with you having a good sense of self-worth. The way we behave when we do not value ourselves is not conducive to authentic friendships. So, if you jumped straight to this chapter with the hope that you'd learn how to make and keep friends, I'd gently suggest you now go back and read the chapter on your relationship with yourself. I promise it's not a therapist copout! It'll support your authenticity and therefore the friends you choose to keep. Speaking to you, personally (not professionally), as someone who struggled to maintain friendships, I can tell you that it all starts with how you feel about yourself.

Step one is do the work on yourself.

Step two of building healthy friendships is to remember that you only need three to five close people in your life and some of those may be family members or your romantic partner, so maybe you only need a couple of really strong friendships. Focus on the quality and levels of intimacy within these friendships rather than worrying about whether you have enough friends.

Step three is to understand your personal processes around the expectations you have of your friends, how you cope with disappointment, and what you do and how you feel in response to real or perceived abandonment and rejection in friendships.

Lastly, it's important to be able to make good decisions about where you put your energy, based on your social arousal needs. There's no point in trying to create a healthy friendship with someone who zaps you of all your energy; in fact, that dynamic may well end up having a negative impact on your mental health.

SUPPORTING FRIENDS THROUGH DIFFICULT TIMES

One of the most common questions I get asked on social media and at speaking events is: How do I support my friend who's going through a difficult time? As a therapist, I tend to lean in when people are having a difficult time, but I understand this is not the norm. I think people genuinely want to know what the right thing to say or do is. And while you might be working on deepening the intimacy in your friendships, I get that along the way it can be a bit of a minefield trying to muddle through difficult times. So, in a rather out-of-character way, I'm going to give you some direct advice here...

My advice largely depends on the context, background and the level of intimacy you already have within the friendship in question, information I do not actually have. But, here are some ideas:

The best place to start is to ask your friend if they need anything or if there's anything you can do. Try not to force help on people, regardless of how close you might be. They may not want it at that time and if you have feelings about that check on your compulsive helping (pp. 75-6). Let them know how available you are to support them (and be honest about it, don't pretend you are 100 per cent available, 24/7) and feel free to ask them if it's okay for you to check in with them if you sense further difficulty or things getting worse. Again they may say 'no thanks' and that's okay too, as maybe, for their own reasons, they have chosen a couple of people to confide in and that select group happens not to include you. You may want to ask if this is the case. Attach no expectation to their response. For some people, receiving help when times are hard is harder than giving it.

When a friend is in need, it can be distressing to witness as well as uncomfortable and frightening, depending on the depth of the issue. It's important to remember that you are having your own set of feelings about what you are witnessing, and you are responsible for managing those feelings. **Tend to your own reaction first and then offer support.**

An example: I had a client once whose very close friend was struggling with self-harm and an eating disorder. In therapy we talked at length about what to say and how to approach the issue. The thing that worked – and by 'worked' I mean supported the friend to get some professional help and helped my client feel he was being active in the situation – was honesty and boundaries.

My client found a way to share his own experience of recover-

ing from mental health and addiction issues, therefore laying the ground for identification, connection and sharing as an equal. He then needed to express his upset about how unwell his friend was becoming and set some firm boundaries to ensure he wasn't, in any way, enabling self-destructive behaviour further. He was then responsible for holding the boundaries he set. Their relationship is now far more distant, but my client is in a healthier space with it.

EXIT STRATEGIES

We've talked mainly about how to maintain and build friendships, but what if you are reading this with a need to shed some friends? Or maybe whilst reading you've realised there are people you'd prefer not to continue in a friendship with. Before we wrap up on this chapter, I'd like to offer you some strategies that can help you to exit a friendship.

Firstly, it's important you are clear on your reason for ending the friendship. Maybe you've realised it's just not a healthy one for you or you simply realise you cannot maintain the number of friendships you currently have with the level of intimacy you'd prefer.

If you do choose to leave a friendship, here are some exit strategies:

Try talking – If you think the friendship is becoming toxic to one or both of you, an honest conversation about it might help in ways that surprise you. When talking, speak in 'I' statements. This ensures you avoid blaming the other person or making assumptions about how they think and feel which can cause further conflict (also see p. 122). Explain which parts of the relationship you are finding hard. Your friend may not have realised and be willing to work on it with you, but if not, talk to them about you needing some space.

Create space – If you are simply trying to reduce your social circle or a conversation is not the way to go, you can create space by waiting longer than usual to respond to messages and phone calls. You can also decline invites, even if you are not busy, to help make some space between the two of you. This will give a non-verbal message that something is not working for you, and you may need to set boundaries if the other person ramps up their contact to try and pull you back in, in order not to 'ghost' them, which is never a good look.

Boundaries – For many people, boundaries feel scary in friendships because you're worried about one of two things: what your friend will think of you, or hurting your friend's feelings. It may also be because you're worried about how it will affect your wider social circle.

If a friend can't tolerate you using your boundaries, it's time to question the basis of the friendship regardless of additional dynamics. You can create boundaries that help you get your wants and needs met in friendships, just as you might do in any other relationship. You can also use boundaries to protect yourself from others by asking them not to contact you and not contacting them in return.

Making the decision to end a friendship is never easy, so how you do it can be quite a sensitive issue. If none of these exit strategies feel like they fit for you, make sure you understand what your motivation is for leaving the friendship. You can try an amalgamation of all three and see which works.

Summary

1. *A friendship is an intimate relationship made up of reciprocation, shared interests, fun, empathy, and any other qualities you would personally add to this list.*
2. *Friendships are a matter of social survival, as infants and as adults. They help prevent feelings of depression, anxiety and stress.*
3. *Friendships are not passive. They take effort to create and maintain.*
4. *You only need three to five close people in your circle, which can include friends, family and romantic partners.*
5. *Adults cannot abandon adults, but they can reject them.*

Chapter Five:
ROMANTIC RELATIONSHIPS

Reflective Question: 'Is it intimacy or is it intensity?'

One of the most important messages I want you to take from this book is that all relationships are worth prioritising. Nonetheless I can't negate that, for a huge number of people, we often feel more content when we have a romantic partner. Consequently, romantic relationships are habitually considered the gold standard that we 'should' be aiming for.

Statistically the average length of a short-term romantic relationship (as opposed to marriage, civil partnerships, and so on) is 3–4 years and 42 per cent of marriages end in divorce – that's nearly half! To state the obvious, if you've been through a breakup or a divorce, it was probably very painful and it probably had an impact on how you felt about yourself and your future romantic relationships too. So, if the stats are almost 50/50, why do we keep doing it? Why is this type of relationship considered the one to be aiming for? If someone told you that getting in a car meant there was a 42 per cent chance you might get hurt, would you do it? Probably not. So why do we keep taking the risk when it comes to romance?

Simple answer: it's biological. We are driven to a) find/create a 'tribe', and b) to procreate so our species can survive. You'll notice that neither of these biological aspects requires us to actually partner up, that part is psychological. As adults, just like when we were children, we need to get our individual attachment and connection needs met in order to survive as individual human entities as well as a species.

But sex and romance never feels that simple, does it?

Sex and romance is, in part, about survival, which is why it feels so good when it goes right and so awful when it goes wrong.

Just like our Family of Origin and our friendships, romantic relationships contribute to our individual psychological survival and the survival of our social status. Romantic relationships also have the potential to move us away from our FOO, if that's what we seek, and fill the relational gaps left over from both family and friendships, and they definitely have an effect on how we feel about ourselves. Romantic relationships are important to us because they have an impact on most areas of our lives, if we let them.

For most of us, how we frame romantic relationships in our minds is based on societal norms that were created a very long time ago. Being a therapist, not a historian, I can't give you the full history of dating. I can, though, offer you some insight and help you to understand the importance of good mental health in romantic relationships, and how to take care of your mental health when relationships don't work out, be that a short-term fling or a long-term partnership. This will involve maintaining your self-worth and holding on to healthy boundaries and learning how to get your needs and wants met. If you would like to explore a history of dating further (it is quite interesting), I recommend you read *Labor of Love* by Moira Weigel (see Further Reading).

The second thing I want to help you do in this chapter is to narrow down the healthy parts of people you are romantically and sexually attracted to, so you don't feel so over- or underwhelmed by who is available.

We'll do a bit less reflecting on your history here than in previous chapters, and instead look at some theoretical options to help you understand how the different parts of someone else impact the different parts of you, layering our work from earlier.

If you are single and on the dating scene, you can use this to inform your choices. If you are in a relationship of any kind that is going well, or not, you can use the same guidance to support the development of healthy intimacy and repair ruptures in order to strengthen your bond.

THE IMPORTANCE OF RUPTURE AND REPAIR IN ROMANCE

In the psychology world, we most often correlate the term rupture and repair with parenting. The word 'rupture' indicates a significant breakdown or stressor on the relationship, regularly evidenced by feelings of betrayal, abandonment and misunderstanding. The 'repair' is the process of acknowledging that there has been a rupture and addressing the disruption to the relationship, hopefully moving you to tackle the fundamental issues and therefore bolstering the trust between you. The concept supports the idea that we are all imperfect, will make mistakes, we all hurt and hurt other people sometimes but in a relationship where the individuals are securely attached it is not the end of the world, it's all repairable. Love, bonding and strong connections are built out of the window of opportunity for healing that ruptures create. Lasting damage is only really done when a rupture is left to fester or occurs repeatedly without the repair.

I'm introducing this concept so early in this chapter because I often meet people who believe they need to be 'perfect' in order to find or keep their romantic partner and more often than not these are the people who are struggling to settle down. They struggle because they attempt to show up for romantic relationships in a perfectionistic adaptation (see page 93) of themselves rather than building a relationship on authenticity and trust. I want to first give you full permission to be messy with romance before we get on to any of the stuff about why you choose the partners you choose. Give yourself space to get things wrong and be imperfect without allowing it to impact your sense of self-worth, something most of us have struggled with in romantic and sexual relationships at some point. I also want to familiarise you with the idea of being accountable for your behaviours, apologising when you get things wrong and taking responsibility for your emotions too, which is hard if you've not had this modelled to you.

If we look at the other types of relationships, the same is applicable. In fact, I would go as far to say that if you can apply the above points across all your relationships, not only will you strengthen your bonds and deepen your intimacy with others, you'll also start to heal the ruptures that haven't been repaired in your own history. And that is ultimately how you begin to end the generational transition of dysfunctional relationship patterns.

If changing generational dysfunction is something you are interested in, it's vital that children born out of current-day relationships are modelled on this type of behaviour. What children see in their parents' relationship teaches them what to expect in their own romantic encounters as they mature. Therefore, parents, spouses or co-parents must actively practise repairing the ruptures between themselves so that children witness it as a normal and functional way of communicating.

Having said that, please don't imagine that I am able to repair every single rupture in my own family with ease. To be really transparent, I tackled some serious ***imposter syndrome*** whilst writing this chapter as I was struggling to repair ruptures happening in my own marriage. It's a really difficult thing to do a lot of the time and can be incredibly upsetting. In practice it can be desperately uncomfortable and sometimes can feel like it punctures our egos. It's a heathy yet vulnerable approach to relating to your partner and your children if you have them, and often we need to find a lot of humility in order to do it.

Where repair simply isn't possible

Despite not having explored trust much in this book, up until now, it is a vital contributor to all relationships. When we place our trust in someone, the love hormone, oxytocin, is activated and makes it conceivable to foster investment in a relationship, as well as prevent depression and anxiety within relationships. When trust is broken, our stress hormones, cortisol and adrenaline, are activated, making repairing the damage challenging as we lose our homeostasis and enter a stress response that in effect hijacks the logical thinking part of our mind. Depending on the individual this can lead to further traumatic stress responses (see p. 136 for the different trauma responses you may experience).

Chapter Five: ROMANTIC RELATIONSHIPS

While I would always support you in attempting the repair if you want your relationship to continue healthily, you are within your rights to consider certain things as bottom lines, meaning that if your partner crosses particular boundaries, repair simply isn't possible and you are not obliged to attempt repair or forgive them.

From working with clients who have felt betrayed in romantic relationships – mostly because their partner started another relationship, slept with someone else or demonstrated behaviour that directly opposed their value system – I know that it can feel really enticing to stay in a relationship despite experiences of betrayal in order to avoid the messiness of the repair or finding out that it's just not possible. If you are unable to find repair and you're left obsessing, ruminating and often distracted by what's happened, months or even years after a betrayal, my very serious question to you would be: What's going on for you that are you maintaining a relationship built on rupture?

Usually, on the surface, it's because of a fear of not finding anyone else, having to 'start again' and on a deeper level it's about a fear of having to move through the full wrath of the horrible emotions and grief that are triggered when we experience a rupture, like a betrayal, that doesn't seem repairable.

In terms of making healthy choices in the first place and to help prevent a betrayal experience, it can be helpful to know what needs and wants you seek to get met in a romantic relationship, and communicate to others exactly what behaviours are off limits inside and outside the relationship(s), also known as 'bottom lines'. For example, affairs aside, my husband communicated very clearly to me that smoking would be the end of our relationship as we know it. As an ex-smoker, knowing the effect it would have on my marriage means I don't entertain the idea of having a cigarette for very long at all.

If you both know and have communicated your needs, wants and bottom lines and they are repeatedly betrayed with no sincere effort to repair the breach of trust the psychological consequences can be dire because, over time, you'll likely lose trust in others and resort to self-sufficiency – where you pathologically and unconsciously push away even those away who are closest to you. So, the impact goes further than the relationship you are in right now. And yet, because we are human, even when this is happening, a drive to find love and trust persists so we can end up experiencing *internal conflict*, a painfully dissonant experience which essentially looks like a difficulty in staying in or leaving relationships.

Cognitive Dissonance

This wouldn't be a psychology book if I didn't offer you at least a little bit of information on cognitive dissonance. The Cognitive Dissonance theories, on which many mental health treatments are founded, were first developed by Leon Festinger in 1956. Essentially, when our thoughts, feelings and behaviours do not match, we experience notable mental stress. Put differently, the mismatch means there is a psychological space created between how we think, feel and behave. If our boundaries and bottom lines have been violated and we stay in a relationship regardless, we are behaving in opposition to how we think and feel and dissonance is created.

Because our nervous systems are always striving for homeostasis (see pp. 99-100 for more), our mind has to find ways of either reducing the amount of difference between our feelings and behaviours by aligning how we think and feel with how we behave, which is usually the goal when we work with cognitive dissonance, or justifying the difference between the two by rejecting any evidence that highlights the dissonance further. My evening chocolate habit is a great example: I know categorically that eating chocolate after dinner disrupts my sleep, it's been proven many times. Sleep is precious to me, I really need it and in general, with a toddler and a baby around, I do not get enough of it, so you'd think I'd be doing all I can to maximise the sleep I can get. And yet I still eat chocolate after dinner. I justify it by telling myself, 'It won't keep me up this time', 'I deserve it, being a mum is hard work' or 'I'll probably be woken up in the middle of the night anyway', and there I have given myself a lovely reason to eat sugar- and caffeine-filled snacks late in the day – only to be kicking myself at 3 a.m. when my blood sugar drops off a cliff and I can't get back to sleep.

We reduce cognitive dissonance in relationships when we've been hurt and let down too many times by moving towards self-reliance and avoiding intimate relationships. This can result in telling ourselves we 'don't need a partner' and come up with other reasons why we should end our search for romantic love or it can be that you continue to search for love via romance but the self-reliance that has formed blocks you from experiencing true intimacy with another person.

In therapy I've noticed several other ways in which people attempt to close the dissonant space in romantic relationships. The main one seems to be a process of adjusting their expectations of what a romantic partner should look like and then adjusting their boundaries around this. It might sound like a solution, but really it is an avoidance tactic and a justification to not experience the difficult feelings that come up when we are experiencing cognitive dissonance. It allows us to continue to put ourselves in situations where we will most likely endure further betrayal – a concept known as ***repetition compulsion.*** The unconscious goal here is that, if we can fix the next betrayal and make things better, we will be able to heal from historical ruptures and betrayals. But it doesn't work. This pattern makes victims of betrayal vulnerable to it happening again. I have only said this explicitly to clients twice in my entire career, as I am not in the business of making other people's life decisions for them, but sometimes the best thing we can do is walk away from a relationship that has proved itself to be irreparable.

WHY DO I SEEM TO ATTRACT/BE ATTRACTED TO A CERTAIN TYPE OF PARTNER?

I've been through a few phases, personally, about who I felt compelled to date – I have mostly been drawn to emotionally avoidant people, although they sometimes came in slightly different aesthetic packages. It was like I could smell avoidance a mile off. In fact, I once had a neighbour who I had never spoken to, but it was as if I could feel his avoidant nature seeping through the walls of our building. I was instantly very attracted to him and ended up 'seeing' him and getting very hurt, more than once. This was one of the experiences that really brought my personal difficulties in romantic relationships to the forefront and made me question the types of people I was choosing to date.

Being attracted to a certain type of person, particularly those who are commitment or emotionally avoidant, is a common experience because so many of us are unconciously afraid of things working out. The older we get the more avoidant people are on the dating scene because, well, they are avoiding relationships, so they are single and those who are attracted to avoidants are also single because the combination tends not to evolve into any type of commitment. If this is the kind of dance you also dance with in romance, I am pleased to tell you that it *is* possible to change who you are attracted to, and one main outcome of doing this work is that who you are attracted to might change without you even noticing. It can change because when we relate to others from a place of self-worth, start taking responsibility for our choices and no longer abandon ourselves, we stop tolerating people who can only offer the crumbs of a relationship and who we find sexy and interesting changes too.

My own story here is just an example. You might be attracted or attracting something completely different. In fact, there are opposing modern-day theories about who we are attracted to – one is that we are attracted to people whose strengths are opposite to ours, so they can make up for our vulnerabilities and us for theirs. The other theory is that we are attracted to people who remind us of ourselves, which some label as ***healthy narcissism***. Have you ever looked at a couple and thought they were quite similar to each other aesthetically? If not, look around... I am sure you'll see it. It can be a signal that the narcissistic part of us is attracted to people who echo ourselves. Take a moment now to reflect on what you feel is true for you.

There's a third contributing factor too – your own history (surprise, surprise). As we covered earlier, some of us will seek relationships outside of our FOO that fill the gaps and allow us to access parts of ourselves that were not permitted or accessible in our family. Others are unconsciously driven to repeat things because somewhere inside us we believe if we repeat a situation enough times, eventually we will be able to repair it and therefore heal the original trauma and past hurts from previous relationships. Which brings us back to repetition compulsion.

Repetition Compulsion
(Trigger warning: rape and sexual violence)
I need to insert a caveat here based on what I told you earlier... the rupture and repair piece only works if you are in a relationship with someone who is psychologically healthy enough to work on things with you. Or if you are able to find ways to repair wounds in your history without your partner's involvement. If you are repeating past traumas by dating people who are not good for you, you won't be able to heal your history internally or externally because you are still re-enacting it.

The repetition compulsion phenomenon can be true for those who find themselves in lots of short-term dating situations, and also for those in longer-term relationships. In longer term relationships it shows up as an ongoing issue or conflict that doesn't seem to resolve itself even over extended periods of time. For example, a couple may find themselves fighting about the same thing over and over. The reason it doesn't seem to change regardless of efforts from either person is firstly, if one partner is unconsciously seeking out intensity and re-enacting historic relational wounds, it's likely that they will have chosen someone who repeats what they haven't repaired, and that's kind of the point, that's what keeps the intensity alive... picking someone who doesn't offer the opportunity to 'fix' history might feel a bit boring and unattractive.

Repetition compulsion also plays out in more obvious ways when there is a history of trauma. Victims of rape or sexual violence might communicate or otherwise indicate that they want to experiment with violence as part of their sex life – just like the example above, they are re-enacting something in an attempt to gain some control over it and potentially repair a feeling of powerlessness, but if they are dating abusive partners as part of their compulsion to replicate things, only the repeat of the rupture is possible, not the repair.

Both anxious and avoidant attachment types engage in repetition compulsion by creating intensity to block intimacy. The anxious person does it more clearly, and somewhat chaotically at times, often by monitoring what the other person is saying, doing and feeling. The avoidant person does it in a more passive way, most commonly through what could be perceived as a lack of effort or interest. The space created by the avoidant person triggers the more anxious person's fears, worries and insecurities, while the intensity coming from the anxious person triggers a need in the avoidant person to back off. Figuring out where the intensity is coming from can feel like a chicken-or-egg type conundrum, although it's most common for the anxious party to take the brunt.

If you can see yourself in any of this, your trauma healing starts with you becoming aware that the excitement you feel when you meet someone new, those butterflies in your belly that we so often confuse with love, *may* actually be your nervous system telling you that something seems unsafe. You have to make the active choice to move away from your attempts to repeat things. That means actively changing direction and opting for peace of mind and intimacy seeking over pleasure and intensity seeking, for now. This could mean not engaging with a specific type of person, or not engaging with a particular topic or behaviour within a relationship. Things may feel a bit boring for a while. They feel boring because, to refer to the reflective question at the start of this chapter, you've been using the intensity created through this process to avoid intimacy.

In that 'boring' (intimate) space, find the opportunity to reconnect with your relationship with yourself (go back to the Self and Family chapters if you need to) and determine what it is you are trying to heal from. When you feel tempted to jump into a relationship, or even just into bed with someone who triggers that feeling in you, or you want to start that fight again, slow down or even stop, go for a walk, meditate or reflect. If it's appropriate to your situation, if you are in an adult state of mind, (see the functional adult exercise on pp. 79-80 for support), and have a partner who is healthy enough to do the work alongside you, have a conversation about what happened, once the emotional charge has died down.

Exercise: Reflections on intensity and intimacy:

Intensity is characterised by an all-consuming feeling that is short lived but somewhat addictive and potentially overwhelming and exhausting.

Intimacy is characterised by being present, vulnerable, mutual. It needs to be earned as it requires trust. It can also feel tiring but productive.

When you consider the reflective question – 'is it intensity or is it intimacy?' – what are your thoughts on your romantic relationships, having read what you've read so far?

Journal your thoughts, or take some time to consider the question.

If you have trouble getting started here are some prompts:
- Three examples of intensity in my romantic relationships
- Three examples of intimacy in my romantic relationships
- When things are intense I feel...
- When things are intimate I feel...

SEX AND LOVE ADDICTION (SLA)

In order to cast a broad enough net, I want to (potentially) introduce you to the concept of Sex and Love Addiction (SLA). Not because I'm here to diagnose everyone who experiences anxious or avoidant behaviours in romantic relationships as a sex and love addict, but because the concept offers a real time structure to understand our feelings and behaviours in romantic relationships without getting bogged down in the psychology of rupture and repair, cognitive dissonance, repetition compulsion etc. This structure can help, at the very least, to reduce the amount of pain you experience and, at the very best, heal you from unhelpful behaviours that get you stuck in relationships that are not good for you and help you choose healthier partners.

Process Addictions Explained

The word 'addict' can bring to mind a caricature of a drug addict living on the streets, and yes, the disease of addiction can take people there. However, addiction comes in many forms and although your mind may hurtle towards things like drugs, alcohol or gambling, there is a whole other side to the addiction sphere, called ***process addictions***.

Process addictions are addictions to things that don't involve chemicals intoxicating us. Instead, our behaviours trigger chemical releases, and we chase a high or euphoric feeling from our own biological reactions. Exercise, shopping, self-harm, money, OCD, eating disorders, work and gambling are all examples of process addictions. In order for it to be classified as an addiction, there must also be repeated behaviour over time despite detrimental consequences. When considering process addictions we also consider the pathological and compulsive avoidance of certain things which are part of the addiction.

In my experience, people specifically do not like the phrase 'sex and love addiction/avoidance' because it brings up further ideas of desperation, sexual crimes and shame. This is usually because the words 'sex' and 'addiction' are being used in the same sentence and both those words, rightly or wrongly, have become associated with shameful behaviours.

It's also important to differentiate that pure sex addiction is something very different to what I'm talking about here. A sex addict needs very specific treatment and is experiencing something different to a sex and love addict. In sex and love addiction, sex is used as a means to an end to get the high sought rather than it being the actual drug itself. The actual drug, in other words, where the high comes from, is the pursuit of love, which for a lot of people involves sex in one form or another. Whereas the sex addict is addicted to sex experience itself.

Diagnosing SLA

Like other addictions, sex and love addiction or avoidance is about escaping from our own psychological *dis-ease* and emotional pain. Despite how it may appear, the other person or people involved are not the drug – it's the mental obsessions, fantasies and rituals that are addictive. Put another way, it's what's going on in your mind that you are addicted to – which is why sex and love addicts are addicted to sex and love avoidants, and vice versa; it's the only way to feed the mental obsession.

Sex and love addiction/avoidance is usually self-diagnosed by the level of negative impact and consequences associated with the behaviour. Like any other addiction, the behaviours and thoughts get progressively worse, you get more obsessive, and your consequences continue to worsen. See the cycle of addiction diagram below:

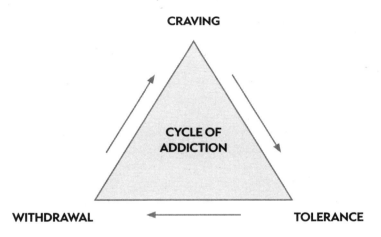

Craving: A yearning for a relationship kicks in, in an attempt to escape difficult emotions.

CRAVING

CYCLE OF ADDICTION

WITHDRAWAL ← **TOLERANCE**

Eventually the relationship, fantasy, sex or obsession stops working and you are plummeted back into your internal world, in which there is pain you only know how to deal with through craving more sex and love.

The more you act out on the symptoms of SLA the less effect they have, so you have to increase the intensity in order to get the same result.

Is it love or is it addiction?
You could argue that, authentic love equals intimacy and addiction equals intensity. But is the feeling of being addicted to someone a part of being in love? Maybe it is. The difference between love (intimacy) and addiction (intensity) when SLA is active is

that we are addicted to the intensity of the chase and the fantasy so we are not intimately or intensely in love with the other person themselves.

Some of you might find it helpful to read that you can be love addicted/avoidant to the gender you are not sexually attracted to and experience a similar set of symptoms. I am heterosexual but most of my early love addiction work was around older women, which was associated with me seeking out a maternal figure in an attempt to heal the wounds inside me connected to my relationship with my mother.

From an early age I developed love-addicted tendencies towards women and avoidant tendencies around men – unless I was dating an avoidant, in which case my love addiction tendencies could be activated around men too. Until I understood the love addiction material, I felt quite confused about the intensity I felt towards older women. When we have very intense feelings in relation to another person, it can be easy to conflate infatuation and an anxious attachment with romance and sexual attraction.

Whatever gender you find yourself love addicted/avoidant around, the tell-tale signs of it being addiction rather than love are:

- Frequent fantasies about the other person
- Obsessive thinking
- Fear of being abandoned
- Fear of intimacy
- Sexualising emotions (meaning that when you're in touch with an undesirable emotion like fear or shame you tend to feel sexual rather than being connected to the emotion itself)
- Magical thinking, in other words, believing the other person is flawless and can make everything feel better for you
- A preoccupation with what the other person is doing
- Repeatedly mistaking casual sexual experiences for healthy intimacy or love
- Abandoning your wants and needs to accommodate a specific person
- Intrusive thoughts related to sex and love

Whether you are in a long-term relationship, are single or dating, it's worth keeping an eye out for any of the above, as they can indicate that there is something in the relational dynamic that is, in the long or short-term, unhealthy and potentially addictive for you. The major giveaway that it is addiction rather than love is that, although the relationship or encounter may feel intensely wonderful at first, when addiction is present there will be harsh consequences, either practically or emotionally to you and/or others.

Conscious and unconscious fears of love addiction and avoidance

Both addiction and avoidance are born out of relational trauma, and these opposing traumas attract each other because they are each trying to resolve something from their history. Having read the section above, you're probably identifying with either the *love addict* or the *love avoidant* (or perhaps both). Here's a more in-depth explanation of each:

Love addicts are usually very dependent on the other person, attempting to enmesh and obsessively care for their partners. Their 'care' is actually about meeting their own needs through monitoring the other person emotionally and practically.

Love addicts are often cognisant of the intensity of emotion (including the pain) that drives their behaviours, and will usually have had a neglectful parent which means they've had to create a fantasy of their ideal caregiver in order to survive. This leads to their using idealist fantasies in adulthood which enables them to tolerate almost anything in romantic relationships. The ability to maintain the fantasy is what makes breaking down the denial and delusion so hard. Even if the love addict is in an objectively abusive relationship, they may be able to justify what's happening by living in the fantasy version of the relationship instead of their reality. However, the fantasy is only effective if they are abandoning their relationship with themselves, ironically doing to themselves what they fear and are desperately trying to prevent the other person from doing.

Put simply: **The Love Addict is consciously afraid of abandonment and unconsciously afraid of intimacy.** The unconscious is significant because it's our unconscious fears that propel us into relationships and situationships that result in emotional pain and trauma, the type that repeats history. The love addict's unconscious fear of intimacy usually plays out in a desperate need to connect with the fantasy of a person who can make everything better and take their pain away for good, filling the gaps or wounds from childhood or past relationships. Love addicts often haven't had good role modelling around what healthy intimacy and indeed boundaries look like, so they do not really know what they need from someone else, which means the person they are relating to will likewise find it impossible to figure out and eventually will withdraw, because they feel that they cannot get anything right or do not have enough to give. Unconsciously they are picking people who won't stay, or they're pushing people away because the intensity of the dynamic that plays out leads them to feel they are not enough for others.

When we are unconsciously afraid of intimacy, because we didn't get the love and approval we needed as children, we don't know how to receive intimacy in adulthood, and we find ourselves attracted to people that, on some level, we know will not stick around – usually a *love avoidant*.

The love avoidant is consciously afraid of intimacy and unconsciously afraid of abandonment. This person usually had an enmeshing or engulfing parent, leading them to a fear of being drained and suffocated in adult relationships. It was their job to caretake their parent's emotions – and consciously or not, they resented it.

Their parent may have *love bombed* them with what looked like generosity and big-heartedness, but the caregiver's behaviour was actually an abandonment of the child's needs, motivated by their own emotional requirements (note the connection to love addiction symptoms above). Even when they are 'just trying to make sure the child is okay', the parent is monitoring the child's emotional experiences and attempting to exert influence so that they can feel worthy themselves. As the child within this dynamic, we learn that our needs are not as important as the person you are in a relationship with, and that we are obliged to take on more responsibility than is appropriate and, more importantly, always appear to be 'okay'. Avoidants are often called cold, mean and distant but they are frightened, and don't know how to express their true emotions. They are avoiding taking the risk of abandonment in the first place, thus sometimes avoiding emotional intimacy altogether.

The love avoidant may use a wall (different to a boundary as it doesn't create intimacy) of artificial maturity. They appear less chaotic and more in control than the love addict, but they are just as scared. They may use sex as a way to avoid being seen for who they are as well as avoiding getting to know the other person. They are unconsciously driven towards the love addict because having someone whose needs appear bigger than theirs is familiar and provides a wonderful reason for them not to express their own needs, allowing them to continue to avoid healthy intimacy.

The self-fulfilling prophecy means that, sooner or later, the love avoidant will feel suffocated and want to get out of the relationship. This is sometimes an attempt to heal their FOO trauma by exerting the power they did not have in childhood. Because of the unconscious fear of abandonment, a love avoidant will do their best to stay in control of situations so that they can tell themselves they are in charge of the ending (when really it's driven by an unconscious fear). This usually looks like them leaving before there is a chance for them to be abandoned or engulfed. In the most extreme cases they are unable to tolerate any kind of need coming from the other person, and they may not know how to leave either. This is where we often see people *gaslighting* and ghosting others as they simply do not have the tools for a healthy or respectful ending.

And yes, you can experience both sides of these conscious and unconscious fears. If you had one parent who was enmeshing and the other neglectful, people you meet who are on the avoidant end of the spectrum will trigger the love-addicted fears in you, while the people you meet who are on the more addicted end of the spectrum may trigger the love avoidant fears within you.

Co-addicted relationships

We use the term co-addicted when a love addict and a love avoidant are together, the result being that the symptoms play out on rotation. The couple may break up and get back together many times, feeling that something is left undone. Usually what is left undone is the healing from their histories.

Occasionally we see two love addicts in a relationship with each other. It is likely that the dynamic will be very fiery and there'll often be arguments, lots of love bombing and emotions will run high. If love avoidants get into a relationship with each other, it's quite likely that they will both avoid intimacy and grow apart by focusing on things outside of the relationship: it is fertile ground for affairs and other betrayals. For more on this see Pia Mellody's *The Intimacy Factor* in Further Reading.

> **Exercise: Changing your attachment styles in adulthood**
>
> *Ultimately these patterns are adult versions of insecure attachment styles. Look back at the attachment styles section on p. 44. Are there any similarities in your childhood attachments (in other words, with your Family of Origin (FOO)) and your adult romantic attachments? How would you like it to be different? What needs to happen for that to be so?*

HEALING

I hope what you've read so far in this chapter helps you to understand the interaction between your adult self in romantic relationships and the historical triggers that can be activated in romantic relationships from your childhood. As well as the important differences between intimacy and intensity.

To summarise: if you suffer emotional deprivation in childhood, you start to develop rituals to mask the ruptures that were never repaired. Although your conscious motivation is to heal, feel better and fall in love, the end results tend to be heartbreak and pain, meaning you continue to re-enact the blueprint that was set in place a long time ago.

Healing in order to develop healthy romantic relationships happens when we're able to turn the wounded younger parts of us, who are seeking love externally, to face our functional adult self (see pp. 79-80) and start to understand that the unconditional love

Chapter Five: ROMANTIC RELATIONSHIPS

we deserve is available from the only person who can really give it... ourselves.

Change and healing happen when we become aware of the unconscious fears that are driving you into unhappy and repetitive relationships. The next exercise, below, will support you in moving away from the love addict/avoidant dynamic, and help you develop healthy communication patterns and intimacy with your partner or future partner.

Most people will never embark on this type of healing because it evokes a grieving process which many of us are resistant to working through, and leads us to admit that who we've chosen (or not chosen) as romantic partners so far has been detrimental to us.

If you were getting into recovery around alcohol, drugs or any other type of chemical addiction, you'd expect a withdrawal period. Clients have often found it helpful to be reminded that in terms of sex and love addiction (SLA) and romance more generally, it's the grief that arises when we change that constitutes the necessary withdrawal on the journey towards healing.

If you've found this section particularly resonates with you and you'd like to find out more about specific healing from SLA symptoms, please see the Further Reading and 'Where to find further support' sections at the end of the book.

Exercise: Finding internal unconditional love

Read the following visualisation exercise before you close your eyes to do it. If it's hard to remember once your eyes are closed, there's a reel on my Instagram account with the same title that you can use as an audio guide instead.

Imagine yourself as a child. How old are you? Who do you seek love from? Scan your mind along your timeline and observe the different ways and people you have attempted to feel unconditionally loved by. This may start with your primary caregivers and move on to romantic partners as the image of your inner child ages.

You will now most likely be aware of a young inner child who sought love from their caregivers and an adolescent or young adult part of you who is trying to navigate romantic relationships. Ask them both to face you, as you activate your functional adult.

First give the adolescent a hug and tell them that you understand them, and you love them unconditionally (or come up with your own phrases if they work better for you). Allow them to stand by your side and hold their hand whilst you take the younger inner child in your arms and tell them they are unconditionally loved... always. Keep that younger inner child in your heart and check in with them daily as to not abandon them further. You are now able to protect these vulnerable parts of you and can start to heal by guiding them towards finding internal unconditional love.

Take It Further

To unconditionally love the parts of us we don't like and that haven't been liked by others is one of the hardest things I've come across. If, when you meet your inner children or inner-parts, you have negative feelings towards them – whether about how they look, how they feel or how they behave – take this as a sign that these parts of you need to be loved the most. First, start an internal conversation with these parts and work on the relationship from there until you feel more fond of them. It's hard to do but it's possible, and it works to teach you that it is possible for all of you to be loved.

'RED FLAGS' IN ROMANTIC RELATIONSHIPS

Whether or not this whole thing about addiction and anxious/avoidant attachments resonates with you, one thing we all seem to talk about these days are 'red flags'. The term is used with the intention of highlighting characteristics in others that cause a stress or trauma response inside you.

We don't always spot 'red flags' at first, particularly in romantic relationships because: a) we may be driven by unconscious fears; b) we are invested in things working out because we feel better about ourselves if someone wants to stay with us; and c) we don't know or don't want to know what our needs and wants are because we fear rejection as a response to them and how to get them met, and so we stay in denial.

Social media posts will give you endless lists of potential red flags, I find this tends to overwhelm people and prime us to focus on the negative. You'll probably find that the majority of the red flags you read about will fit into the categories below. What you'll notice about these four categories is that they are about your interaction with the other person, and not entirely about the other person as an individual.

The four categories of 'Red Flags' to look out for, at least in my opinion are: trust, authenticity failure, self-esteem changes, and boundary failures and violations. Let's look at each of these in turn:

TRUST ISSUES – A feeling that you can't trust them
Do you ever get the urge to look through their phone? Or want to find out every detail about where they've been, and who they've been with? Urges like this mean you do not trust the other person.

I am currently working through this issue with several clients who are trying to figure out whether it is a red flag or whether it is their own psychology getting in the way of a relationship that could be great – which is always possible, particularly in highly stressful periods of life and if you have a history of being dishonest yourself. Although as a therapist, it's my job to support people in gaining awareness and making their own decisions, I can share from a personal perspective, whenever I have felt suspicious and untrusting of someone or something, I have been proven to be right. So, for me, feeling you can't trust someone is a red flag.

AUTHENTICITY FAILURE – Feeling like you can't be authentically you
Do you feel that your reality changes? Do you abandon yourself? Do your decisions about what you do, who you see and even how you behave rely on what you think the other person might want or how they'll think of you? You might feel controlled by the other person.

Finding yourself in a relationship where you lose connection to your authenticity is an issue. As with adult friendships, you need to know yourself first and understand why any roles you play or adaptations you've created show up in relationships and then choose who to be in a romantic relationship with. Ideally, it's a relationship where all the parts of yourself are accepted, good, bad and indifferent. The relationship may even highlight parts of you that haven't been witnessed before. If you don't feel it's heading in this direction, there's a red flag.

SELF-ESTEEM CHANGES – Your self-esteem takes a hit
Does all that work you've done on learning to like and even love yourself seem to crumble when you are relating to the other person?

Romantic relationships should give you a sense of confidence about yourself. Although your self-worth needn't be effected, if you are feeling 'less than' or 'more than' more often than you are feeling equal to the other person in a romantic relationship, it's a red flag.

BOUNDARY FAILURES AND VIOLATIONS – Your boundaries are being violated or you can't seem to hold them in the first place
Whether you haven't felt able to set boundaries in the first place or you've tried to put internal and/or external boundaries in place, which include sexual boundaries, and they are being ignored.

Sometimes we need to be a little flexible and leave room for compromise, but if you are attempting to set boundaries and feeling ignored or violated on more than one occasion, that's a red flag!

Exercise: Trusting your internal red flags

What emotions do you experience when your nervous system is trying to tell you a relationship is unsafe? I would suggest that any of the following might be indicators: fear, shame, jealousy, distrust.

What behaviours do you observe in yourself? Are you trying to fix things or change another person? Do you go through their personal belongings or engage in internet stalking?

The feelings and behaviours you've identified are your internal red flags – take note of them and decide what action needs to be taken.

Chapter Five: ROMANTIC RELATIONSHIPS

Yellow and Green Flags

Yellow and green flags are all too often pushed aside in the face of red flags. And in our age of social media memes and dating apps, it makes sense that we sometimes develop a negativity bias, meaning we focus on what is wrong and what needs changing or fixing. We give red flags the majority of our attention, instead of focusing on what works well – which can make it difficult to find romantic partners and give them a chance in the first place.

Put simply, yellow flags are behaviours, feelings and dynamics that you can work on, and green flags are things that you consider to be to your liking and would want to maintain.

Here are some examples of green flags in relationships:

- You feel supported
- You feel safe
- You feel you can be honest with them without risk of being attacked
- You feel celebrated
- You feel held in mind
- You feel energised after spending time with them
- Your boundaries are respected
- They show up either practically or emotionally when you need them
- They value your thoughts and opinions
- You can be comfortable in silence with them

And here are some examples of yellow flags (things that can be worked on):

- You find their anger difficult to be around
- You don't have that much in common
- You don't always feel comfortable in their company
- There are some values that don't align with yours
- Your social circle, or theirs, has too much impact on the relationship
- You notice you often expect the worst in the relationship
- Envy, jealousy and resentment
- You don't feel you can confide in them when you are vulnerable

Note: Even if a relationship is made up of yellow and green flags, it still requires work. Becoming passive in your relationships can in fact create red flags that weren't there to begin with.

I invite you now to take a moment for reflection on the parts of your relationship(s) or past relationships that are good enough just as they are, even if there are far less of them than the bits you want to change. Take a moment to appreciate and be grateful for the positive because, even if your current situationship doesn't work out as you imagined, you'll have it logged in your mind somewhere that someone, at some point, demonstrated the right flags for you.

UNDERSTANDING YOUR ROLES AND DYNAMICS IN ROMANTIC RELATIONSHIPS

The following sections offer some theoretical insight into the roles we play and dynamics we find within romantic relationships. They'll support you to think about who you are choosing to spend your time and energy on, and offer ways in which you may tweak and repair things in order to change who you're attracted to and create healthier bonds.

Transaction Analysis (TA)

Transaction Analysis (TA) is a psychoanalytic theory created by Eric Berne that helps identify *ego states*. So rather than looking at your entire childhood, you can group the parts of yourself which you know exist into three categories. It can make things feel more manageable within the complexities of romantic relationships.

According to Berne's theory, the three ego states are:

- *Adult* – active when your thoughts and feelings are contextual to the current situation. Engaging in logical thinking and problem solving.
- *Parent* – active when your thoughts and feelings are maternal or paternal. Can be either nurturing or critical. Behaviours that you may have picked up from parents, or when you are in a 'trying to teach someone a lesson' state of mind.

Chapter Five: ROMANTIC RELATIONSHIPS

- *Child* – active when your thoughts and feelings are reminiscent of childhood or are coming out in a childlike way.

In an adult romantic relationship, the ideal form of connection and intimacy is adult to adult. This means that we are present and responding to each other in the here and now. Sometimes, though, what happens is that our parent or child ego states are activated. We essentially start responding from our history and there's a phrase **'if it's hysterical, it's historical'**, which means we are no longer present and intimate with our partner and we are not responding contextually as an adult, we are creating intensity instead.

To take a common example: arguing about the washing up. Let's face it, in the grand scheme of things, it doesn't really matter how the washing up gets done as long as it gets done, and no one is harmed in the process. Nevertheless I've worked with a number of couples who find the way their partners do or don't do the washing up a trigger for their parent or child ego state. This generally happens because one partner is a 'clean-up as they go' type of person, while the other lets the mess build up and is happy to clean up later on. So, when the person who prefers to clean up as they go sees a kitchen full of crockery yet to be cleaned, their critical parent ego state might be activated. They could start feeling angry and telling the other person that the way they do things is wrong, with their attitude being 'my way is better, learn from me'. Alternatively, their child ego state could be activated and they could slip into a victim role or a psychological place that feels childlike, their catchphrase being something like 'Why are you doing this to me? You're so annoying'.

What this scenario offers is an opportunity to repair something at both surface level and on a deeper level. But you have to reframe it from a fight you can win into an opportunity for change.

Using this example about the washing up, the repair conversation in adult-to-adult ego states might sound something like this:

Adult 1 – 'I am a "clean-up as you go" type person and you prefer to let chores build up because you're happy to do them before you go to bed. It's quite hard for me to tolerate because I prefer a clear space. Can you try and explain to me why your way works better for you so I can work on understanding my feelings about it?'

Adult 2 – 'I know you find it annoying when you come into the kitchen, and I haven't cleared up. I am often prioritising other things – like taking our child out for some fun or making sure I am on time for my next meeting – so I prefer to do the washing up later on.'

Adult 1 – 'I can understand that you're prioritising different things and I need you to understand that one reason I feel annoyed about it is that it's difficult for me to use the kitchen throughout the day if you don't clear up as you go. I often feel I have to do your clearing up so that I can make space to cook dinner. It's like you're not considering that I live here too.'

Adult 2 – 'That makes sense to me. Maybe we could compromise?'

Adult 1 – 'Yes, what would be helpful for you?'

Adult 2 – 'It seems like, if I were to put my stuff in the sink or dishwasher straight away rather than on the kitchen surfaces, that would mean you had space to use the kitchen and I can still do my washing up a bit later.'

Adult 1 – 'I think that sounds good.'

This very scripted conversation supports you to stay in an adult ego state and demonstrating empathy and effort to understand each other's actions and reactions – and that is where the repair happens. This process will not only strengthen the bond with your partner and allow you to maintain healthy intimacy; it will also touch on any wounds that need repair inside you where someone did not take the time to understand your thinking before they criticised, challenged or corrected you.

Although I've offered you the script above, the truth is that arguments about washing up are rarely about the washing up. More often, the content is a metaphor for the messy and unprocessed material within the couple. For example, maybe the person who

Chapter Five: ROMANTIC RELATIONSHIPS

cleans up as they go would prefer to spend some quality time with their partner and it angers them that the time at the end of the day is spent cleaning rather than hanging out and being intimate with each other – but you probably won't get to that unless you deal with the surface washing up issue as adults.

Once you've got an understanding about the washing up – or, insert any other reoccurring domestic conflict here – and the ego states that are activated, you need to deal with the quality time and intimacy issue. If you don't, the washing up issue will keep happening in various guises of parent to child interactions.

It takes a lot of strength to stay in the adult part of yourself and attempt a repair if your partner is responding from a child or parental ego state. It is very easy to slip into an unhelpful dynamic and usually we end up on what is known as Karpman's Drama Triangle (see below).

Before I start talking about that, I want to add that fighting is sometimes the adult and healthy thing to do. You don't need all your adult-to-adult conversations to be scripted and robotic like the one above and you don't need one hundred per cent of your conversations to be adult-to-adult. Expressing raw and unprocessed emotion can be a very helpful signal that you feel overwhelmed yet safe enough to be true to yourself within the relationship. It can cause a rupture which then offers an opportunity to heal and repair.

The Drama Triangle (DT)

As you continue to unpack your behaviours in romantic relationships, Steven Karpman's Drama Triangle (DT) is a great resource and it compliments the TA theory covered previously. For information purposes, Karpman was a student of Eric Berne, so the two resources very much go hand in hand and can be applied across most relationship types.

The DT is a concept that has never gone out of fashion; therapists have used it to help their clients since its invention. It describes three unconscious psychological drives that develop within relationships to avoid conflict, intimacy and ultimately responsibility for our feelings by creating intensity instead. It can play out anywhere (including inside your own head) but we'll focus on what happens when it occurs within sex and romance.

The Drama Triangle

- Feels sorry for themselves
- Invites rescue
- Is dependent on others
- Does not make decisions
- Stays passive at all costs
- Appears helpless, powerless and hopeless

VICTIM

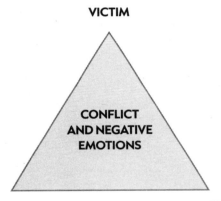

RESCUER

- Plays the hero role
- Is overly responsible
- Appears strong and capable
- Enables others' dependency
- Is self-serving
- Feels sorry for others
- Becomes persecutory if their rescue is not well received

PERSECUTOR

- Controls others through guilt
- Bullies self and others
- Does not own their mistakes
- Appears invulnerable
- Or uses vulnerability to gain power
- Tells others they were wrong
- Shifts shame, blame and judgement onto others

Chapter Five: ROMANTIC RELATIONSHIPS

Frequently we jump on the DT when we experience negative emotions, most commonly anger and conflict. Someone once said to me that without anger and without conflict you cannot authentically love. I thought it odd at the time but as I have matured, I agree. Anger is one of the most important emotions in intimate relationships. It tells us where our boundaries need to be, so it creates intimacy and if we are avoiding it, all we get is intensity. To be in a healthy love relationship we have to be able to express our anger contextually and we need to feel safe coping with conflict and be accountable for it (see p. 146 if you need reminding why).

As in TA, there are unconscious roles you can move into: Victim, Persecutor and Rescuer.

The Victim is someone who feels victimised, sad, helpless, hopeless, powerless and therefore blameless. Their main defence against taking responsibility for their feelings, conflict and intimacy is that they project a sense of vulnerability so that people assume they are too fragile and can't handle other people being angry with them. The victim breeds difficult feelings, including resentment, in others by inviting rescue but not receiving it because they are intent on staying in the victim position.

The way out of the victim position is to take a self-inventory within the relationship you are concerned about and look honestly at what you are doing that keeps you there. To be clear, I am not referring to incidents where you have been a victim of neglect or abuse, that's very different. I am talking about you becoming accountable and responsible for your feelings and the behaviours within romantic relationships that contribute to dysfunction and toxic patterns. At first you may experience shame and anger in response. But that is not a bad thing; it is an indication of the feelings you are repressing and defending against by staying in the victim position.

The Rescuer in its most extreme form is the hero, martyr, caretaker and enabler. Rescuers need victims in order to maintain their position, since their self-worth is often non-existent without someone to save or fix. Unconsciously the rescuer is frightened of being alone, so they have to be a caretaker in order to ensure people stick around and so they can feel better about themselves; their self-esteem is reliant upon it. The rescuer needs to be needed.

If you are stepping in to 'fix' people, relationships or conflicts, when you haven't been asked to, you are effectively forcing your help onto others, and you are in dominant compulsive helping territory (see pp. 75-6). Usually, the expectation of the rescuer is that by eternally helping everyone else, someone will notice when they are in a bad spot and come and save them (so they briefly slip into a victim role), but people tend not to attempt to rescue rescuers because they project themselves as someone who can handle anything. There isn't space for someone else to step in and care for them, a painful dynamic to be involved in.

One way to recover from the rescuer position is to start asking people if they want your help before you try to help them. If they say no, it's likely that you'll feel both anger and shame because those are the feelings you've been avoiding and repressing (just like in the victim role). You then have to do the self-esteem work within your relationship with yourself as well as with your partner. See suggestions on pages 153-4.

The Persecutor is the person who criticises, bullies, shames, punishes and abuses others. They often have a history of abuse themselves, so are full of carried shame; they are re-enacting what was done to them. They have been so hurt that their only option has been to create a defence of anger and persecutory behaviour so that no one can get to them, and no one will see them vulnerable, ever. Although all the roles are about feeling in control, the persecutor role looks like it's the most controlling.

At some point, most people who default to the persecutor role start to feel a sense of guilt about their behaviour. It can go one of two ways. Either they convince themselves this is exactly how it needs to be and continue as they are, or their guilty feelings will shift them into the rescuer role.

When we persecute others, we do it because something happened to us that hurt us and made us feel very small. We carry those feelings into other relationships. Moving away from the

Chapter Five: ROMANTIC RELATIONSHIPS

persecutor role means becoming able to tolerate your anger without blaming others. You realise you are not actually angry at other people as often as it may seem; instead you're angry and hurt with something that's going on inside of you.

I've worked with therapists who teach about the Drama Triangle and offer ways to 'get off it' using feedback loops and loosely scripted conversations. While these things are very useful, for me the hard and fast way to bust the dysfunctional communication that happens when you and your partner are 'drama triangling' is to name it. Name it, see it, expose it – and take a pause. If your partner is familiar with the concept, say this out loud: 'We're on the drama triangle, let's pause for a second.'

A lot can happen during the pause, which can last just a few seconds or more if you need it to: one partner may continue with the DT; they may stay in the role they've already been playing out, or they may switch to another role in an attempt to draw you back in... But regardless, take your pause. If the pause feels hard it might be because the main function of the roles is to avoid increased responsibility. By increased responsibility I mean taking full responsibility for your thoughts, feelings and behaviours as well as your history, something many of us avoid. And if you want healthy romantic intimacy, you have to be prepared to take responsibility for all the parts of you – past and present – along with all the emotions you have – high and low and how you respond to your partner. The act of pausing offers a moment to reflect and self-soothe, which can feel like a challenge, if you're set on avoiding your own internal world. Although I wrote this before I knew about it, research which was released in August 2024 evidenced that this method of temporarily delaying or pausing, whether forced or elective, can reduce the negative impact of any aggression happening between couples (See Further Reading).

Here is another diagram with my take on some healthy alternatives to the Drama Triangle:

Healthy Alternatives to the Drama Triangle

- Identify and express your needs
- Practise using your words
- Take emotional risks
- Acknowledge your strengths
- Accept your vulnerabilities
- Ask for help
- Know that feeling uncomfortable is okay

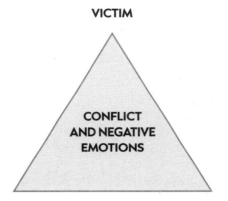

VICTIM

CONFLICT AND NEGATIVE EMOTIONS

RESCUER

- Express your concerns for others
- Invite equality
- Nurture and guide others
- Work on your empathy
- Ask others if they want help first
- Practise setting boundaries
- Don't do for others what they can do for themselves

PERSECUTOR

- Create structure
- Set limits for yourself
- Communicate assertively
- Practise active listening
- Be accountable to yourself
- Ask more questions
- Make your expectations very clear

We move into these roles unconsciously to defend against vulnerability, conflict and undesirable emotions. We do not know we are doing it, until we realise. Once we become aware of how we play these roles within our romantic relationships, and what historical experiences or trauma triggers that behaviour in us, it's our responsibility to try and stay off it by using our awareness (prompted when we take a pause) and choose healthy intimacy over intensity.

> *Exercise: Check in on your Mental Health in Romantic Relationships*
>
> *Below are some reflective questions to help you check on how things are going in your current sexual or romantic encounters.*
>
> *Relationship with yourself* – *How do you value yourself in relation to romantic partners? Do you generally see yourself as better than them or less than them? Do you tend to merge and enmesh with them? Do you lose yourself a bit and take on their likes, dislikes, views and opinions?*
>
> *Holding Boundaries* – *How do your boundaries change when romance gets involved? Do you let romantic or potential romantic partners push boundaries you hold strong in other types of relationships? For example, with friends maybe you wouldn't tolerate lateness, cancelling plans or lying without saying something about it, but in romantic relationships would you let these things slide?*
>
> *Authenticity* – *How capable are you of holding onto your reality and your truth when a romantic partner challenges it? Do you fall in line with who they want you to be and find yourself agreeing with and agreeing to things that ordinarily you wouldn't? Do you change who you are to suit the other person?*

CREATING HEALTHY INTIMACY IN ROMANTIC RELATIONSHIPS

It's the thing we all seek – an intimate, loving and functional relationship with someone we've chosen and who has chosen us from a healthy place. For the remainder of this chapter, I will be offering you practical ideas on how to change how and who you are relating to in romantic relationships.

Here are my top six signs (building on the green flags shared earlier) that a relationship is healthy:

1. All parties are working on communicating, connecting and understanding ways that work for everyone involved.
2. Trust is rarely doubted.
3. Self-esteem is supported, self-worth is never tested.
4. Boundaries are respected.
5. All parties are open and willing to be kindly challenged.
6. There are disputes and they get fully dealt with.

Let's break these six points down a bit further:

1. Communication, connection and understanding really is the single most important factor in building healthy romantic intimacy. I'm positive I am not the first person to tell you this, and I'm also positive that you know it's much harder to do than it is to write. It's hard to do because we all communicate and connect in different ways and we all understand and need to be understood in different ways too. In addition, all three concepts need to work in tandem; you can communicate all you like, but if you are not connecting and understanding each other it's just words with no real intimacy to back them up.

If you know about 'love languages', you'll know that marriage counsellor Gary Chapman coined five types of communication in romantic relationships: words of affirmation, gifts, acts of service, quality time and physical touch. His book *The Five Love Languages* points out that you have to make an effort to speak to your partner using *their* love language – not yours. If there are different love languages being used as efforts for connection, things can be easily misunderstood and relationships can break down – because one or both people feel disconnected and under-appreciated.

Healthy communication means meeting in the middle. I don't believe it's possible to completely change how we communicate, but it can be tweaked to align with your current partner, and it's the effort that really matters. If you know they need to hear that you love them (words of affirmation) and you need them to show you that they love you (acts of service), understand that on some days, as a couple, you may swing more towards one communication style and on other days towards the other. This stands even when you are angry and in conflict. You aim to respect the relationship and each other by continuing to work on communicating, and in ways that help both of you to understand each other.

Keep an eye out for the bids your partner makes for understanding, connection and communication. Their 'bid' might be as subtle as bringing up a topic for conversation or making you a meal, or as overt as initiating sex and lavishing you with gifts. Get sensitive to it – you may not be as interested in the topic they bring up as they are, but your engagement with it is what allows the communication to flow, the love to grow and the connection to follow. Likewise, you may not feel like having sex every time they initiate, but acknowledging it as a request to feel close to you can ensure emotional needs are being met, even when sexual ones can't be. If you're interested in finding out what your love language is, check out *Love Languages* in the Further Reading section.

Just before we move on, I would add that, in my view, there can be more than the original five choices that Chapman lays out for us. Understanding each other's trauma could also be considered a love language, for example, as could giving someone space when they need it, demonstrating interest and concern about a person's situation can also communicate love. But on the whole, Chapman's chosen five tend to cover most things within romantic relationships.

Exercise: Experimenting with communication, connection and understanding

This week, make a list of all the ways your partner communicates with you. Keep it somewhere safe, and if you begin to feel disconnected, remind yourself of their communication style (or love language) and see if it helps you to feel more communicative, connected and understanding.

2. Trust: Trust is usually harder for people who grew up with an emotionally dishonest parent who would, for example, say one thing but mean another. Or an engulfing parent who offered endless generosity in order to meet their own emotional needs rather than yours. Trust is also harder in romantic relationships where you met your partner in a dishonest way, be that relationships overlapping or any other type of physical or emotional dishonesty.

In terms of earning and building trust in a romantic relationship, sometimes it's as simple as trusting a partner as long as they have never done anything to damage your trust. But it's not always that easy. Depending on what you've been through in your life, you may withhold trust for longer and need people to earn it, and that's fine too. If your relationship is going well, look for evidence that you can trust – particularly if you've had a rough ride as you may have become prone to self-sufficiency and negative expectations, and want to retrain your mind to focus on something more positive (see the mindfulness exercise below for support on this). Having said that, if your gut is telling you that something isn't quite right, then listen to yourself. Also, just a tip – do a check-in regarding the other parts of your life – relationships, work, self-care, parenting, and so on – and see if anything else outside the relationship might be impacting your ability to trust that you could be projecting or transferring on to your romantic partner.

The hard and fast truth is that we create trust when we are honest. In Chapter One, I talked about the importance of being honest with yourself (pp. 27-9). If you are honest with yourself, you'll find it easier to be honest with other people, which builds trust in yourself and also in your relationships.

Exercise: Mindfulness

When you've had a difficult time with romantic partners – whether you've been broken up with, cheated on, ghosted or experienced abusive relationships – it is very normal to focus on the negative and look for reasons not to trust as well as being stuck in a fantasy of the future or trying to change the narrative of the past. It's how your mind protects you from getting hurt again.

Chapter Five: ROMANTIC RELATIONSHIPS

If you believe you are now safe and/or in a relationship and your mistrust is coming from inside you rather than something the other person is doing, you can practice mindfulness in order to gain more control over where your thinking goes. I cover mindfulness in much more depth in my first book, Your Mental Health Workout.

Here are some really easy practical steps to get you started:
- *Assign a time each day where you can take between 1 and 5 minutes (longer if you wish) for yourself.*
- *Observe your breathing patterns.*
- *Each time you notice your mind wandering (and it will do), bring it back, in a gentle way to continue focusing on your breathing patterns.*
- *Repeat for your chosen amount of time.*

Over time, this remarkably simple exercise trains your mind to choose what to focus on.

Take It Further

In a healthy relationship, work on letting go of the negative thoughts about your relationship, and choose to focus on the positive things that will support you to feel trusting and trustworthy.

3. Self-Esteem: This, and self-worth, are never more confronted than in romantic relationships, because the parts of us that seek unconditional love are activated.

I have found that my most effective way of working on self-esteem within sexual and romantic relationships is to use mantras and affirmations exceptionally often, it's worked really well for both me personally as well as for my therapy clients. Here are some that have been created in sessions with me recently:

- My value is not dependent on how they respond to me
- I am the best person I know
- Be more [insert your first name]
- All areas of my life are working well, and this encounter does

not affect them
- My self-talk is positive and loving
- My relationship does not define me
- I am worth fighting for

As a reminder, affirmations and mantras are not there to make you feel better in the moment, although that might happen. Their role is to shift how value yourself on a much deeper level, and that only happens when you commit to them. I usually suggest picking one affirmation and repeating it several times a day for a week and see what happens. See *Your Mental Health Workout* in Further Reading for an in-depth look at getting affirmations working for you.

Exercise: Create your own relationship mantras and affirmations

Technical pointers:
1. *They are always positive*
2. *They are always done with compassion*
3. *They are ideally in the present tense*

Think about this as an equation:
Feelings + Needs (or Wants) = Mantra

Reflect on how you felt in your most recent romantic interaction. Identify your feelings and what they are telling you about what you want and need. Use this information to create a baseline mantra.

For example:
'I feel sad that they don't want to see me for a second date. I need some time to process it and a big hug from someone I know cares for me.'

The above feelings and needs could be translated into the mantra:
'I value my space and I always deserve comfort.'

Chapter Five: ROMANTIC RELATIONSHIPS

4. **Boundaries:** These should always be placed out of love, not through bitterness or as an attempt to manipulate the other person. Healthy boundaries are malleable and changeable, dependent on the situation in hand, see page 39 for a reminder.

In a healthy relationship you may not agree on a specific boundary, but if it's important to one person it needs to be important to the other. That means, even if you are annoyed by the boundary, you respect it. Just make sure your boundaries are boundaries and not walls or orders:

Walls	Boundaries
Do not talk to me like that.	When you talk to me like that, I can't respond from a functional place. Let's talk about it later.
Don't call me before 9 p.m.	I can't speak earlier than 9 p.m. because I'm putting my kids to bed.
Go away.	I need some space, let's talk tomorrow.
Don't comment on how I look.	It makes me uncomfortable when you comment on my appearance.
You're scaring me!	I don't feel safe right now – please lower your voice.
I am not talking about this anymore.	This topic is no longer up for discussion.

5. **Challenging:** To challenge a romantic partner feels scary because it may tap into an infant felt sense – one where, if you didn't satisfy, please or placate your caregivers, your survival was threatened. In addition, if your caregivers were angry a lot of the time, you may sense that you are doing something wrong when you need to

challenge someone. I can summarise that, as I have done previously on social media by saying, **If we are taught that we will only be deemed lovable by satisfying and placating others, then we learn that attention is more valuable than respect, and pleasure is worth more than love.** Consequently, as adults, most of us refrain from challenging our romantic partners.

Talking to a partner about something you don't think is right, or something you'd just like to be different, takes a lot of courage, as does receiving the challenge. In a healthy relationship, challenging each other will still feel confrontational but shouldn't feel antagonistic; you're on the same side! Challenging each other ideally works to strengthen the bond. Nonetheless, challenges can also lead to disputes…

Exercise: Pick Your Battles

When something comes up that you feel you need to challenge – before you jump straight in – give it a rating:

A rating of 1 for things that, at the end of the day, are not going to have a huge impact, such as: toothpaste on the mirror or used tissues not being put in the bin; and a rating of 10 for things that have serious consequences, such as: sexual behaviour you're uncomfortable with, violence, theft, or anything that touches on abuse or neglect.

If you rate your current dilemma above a 4, challenge it. Below a 4, take some time to decide if your feelings are really about the challenge you want to make, or if there's something else going on that you could be more honest about.

6. Disputes: Disputes and arguments are a really strong part of a healthy relationship, and help you get to know each other better. They tell you about where your boundaries are. You should be able to feel angry with your partner and safe at the same time, and also know that it will pass, and that the relationship will survive.

A healthy relationship allows space for strong feelings to surface, and then, when the emotional charge has passed a little, there will be

Chapter Five: ROMANTIC RELATIONSHIPS

room for communication, where you can challenge each other and explore opportunities to rebuild or strengthen the trust between you. While I was writing this book, my husband and I had the mother of all disputes. I found myself throwing his shoes out of the front door, and trying to push him out of the house... If you needed evidence that what we know in theory does not always help when emotions are running high, now you have it.

After that fraught morning, once our toddler was napping, we had a long, tearful, conversation. Fundamentally, the fight we were having was because we were showing love in different ways and missing each other's bids for connections. We were neglecting to find time to keep each other up to date with how we were and things that were bothering us that could lead to further disputes.

Like many couples when we get into a dispute, we tend to be fighting about different things, which is why, even if your intention is to be working on all of the above, it's so hard to resolve. He is focused on logic, and I am focused on emotion. I am upset about the impact something has had on me over a period of time, while he is set on saying that I am not being fair because it wasn't his intention, and he is doing his absolute best (which, when I am not in a heightened state of emotion, I entirely believe) and can be left feeling triggered around his belief that his best isn't good enough. I often focus on unresolved themes from the recent past that have built up, and he is focused on the current situation and context alone. In these situations, we are not communicating, we are reacting.

After this particular argument we agreed, to the best of our ability, to take five minutes each per day to talk through anything that was building up internally and to speak about what kind of day we'd had. During each other's five minutes, the other one is not to respond (which is so hard!), though they can respond afterwards, or reflect on what's been said and respond at a later date. In reality it was difficult to do this every single day, and it fell by the wayside after a few weeks, only to be reinstated after another big fight. I found it really helpful to voice my thoughts and feelings each day. My husband found it hard. So, we had to compromise and do it a few times a week rather than every single day.

One thing to be aware of with this approach: if you want a response to something you've said within your five minutes – you need to ask for it. Your five minutes is your protected time to say what you need, what you've noticed and how you've felt about things that have happened. The other person has no obligation to pick up on things or reply, so if you need or want more conversation about something, ask for it. If like me, you're the one who feels the emotional benefits more, then you will probably need to initiate this exercise too.

Note: At times during the lifespan of a relationship, challenging each other and even giving constructive feedback is just not helpful – for example, if a new baby has arrived, a family death has occurred, or if someone's been made redundant. These are all times for nothing but support and compassion.

Communication techniques

Whether you've just started dating and you want to set things up well, or if you've been in a long-term relationship or are even married, these techniques will support you and your partner(s) to be happy and healthy within the relationship and allow space for conflict and healing. You can use them in all other relationships, too.

Use 'I' statements – Always talk in the first person when you are talking about yourself. Far more often than we are aware, we depersonalise things by using 'you', 'they' or 'one' instead of 'I'. We also tend to tell other people what we are thinking about them rather than how we feel about what's happening. It's a socially acceptable way of disconnecting from your reality, and prevents you from the uncomfortable feelings that come with being transparent and owning your authenticity which we want you to feel so that you can practise communicating with them and build the intimacy within the relationship.

Concentrate on talking about your thoughts and feelings by starting your sentences with 'I'. You will feel vulnerable and uncomfortable. Listen to the emotions that are activated: they are there to guide you and tell you what's important to you and what you need. This will help you to be more in tune with your nervous system too, and it will help create trust internally and externally.

Don't say the words 'you make me feel' – This is the *only* point in this book where I will categorically say 'Don't do that'! Telling someone that they make you feel something, particularly something negative, introduces the opportunity for a huge emotional charge. It

Chapter Five: ROMANTIC RELATIONSHIPS

discharges the emotional responsibility on to the other person. For example: 'You make me feel like a terrible wife' or 'You make me feel rejected when you don't reply to my texts' blames the other person for how *you* feel. Instead, try 'I feel like a terrible wife when you say that.' It will feel far more vulnerable because it's closer to the truth, and you are holding on to your emotional duty within the relationship, which helps create vulnerability and healthy intimacy.

Even when it's positive, saying 'You make me feel' can, at times, have a negative impact, because the responsibility to continue making you feel that way is passed over. Instead, try 'When I am around you I feel important/loved/valued/sexy' and so on.

Listen... to yourself – Earlier we talked about ego states, and part of healthy communication is knowing which part of yourself you are communicating from. Listen to yourself when you communicate. How old do you sound/feel? Are you communicating from an adult ego state? Or is one of your inner children in the driving seat? Of course, listen also to the other person – you can use the active listening exercise from pp. 81-3 to support you in listening and hearing each other accurately.

Stay interested – This comes up a lot when I see one half of a couple in a long-term relationship that has become difficult. They say, 'They're not interested in me anymore', to which I usually ask, 'Are *you* interested in you?' That question usually stumps people a little; they are expecting me to ask if they are interested in their partner, to which they already have a ready, formed answer – usually, *'Yes, of course'*.

Yes, it's important to stay interested in what your other half is doing, but it's equally important to retain an interest in yourself so that you can accurately stay connected and communicate how you are and what you're up to. If you lose interest in yourself within a relationship, if you don't think you are interesting and of value, sooner or later it will rub off on your partner. Losing interest in yourself can also be a symptom of a bigger mental health issue like depression, so it's really worth staying self-aware around this one.

Ask what support is needed – After my husband and I had our first baby, we let our monthly relationship check-in meetings (yes, you read that correctly, this man definitely knows he's married to a therapist) fall off the table. When we finally got round to talking to each other about what was going on between us, we realised that we were not supporting each other enough. Instead, we felt annoyed, isolated, resentful, aggressive, and many more negative things towards each other with very little positive to balance it out. Rather than constantly correcting and challenging each other and jumping on the Drama Triangle, we quite simply agreed to add the following question: 'What support do you need around this?' and the statement 'What I would have found helpful is...'. It really helped, and I'd recommend trying it. It can sometimes feel a little forced, but better that than returning to a state of resentment and loneliness within the relationship. You might even want to combine these to follow up the 'five minute each' exercise.

> *Exercise: Pause and Respond*
>
> *Earlier I explained the benefits of pausing when emotions are running high and in the Further Reading section there is new research to back this up.*
>
> *For the next week (or what feels like a realistic stretch of time) commit to pausing before you respond, each and every time that you interact with your partner. Consider if you are responding with any amount of contempt. The amount of self-awareness that can happen in that one moment is phenomenal. Try and you'll see.*
>
> *Check on your inner children. Check that you're responding from your adult self. Double-check on any conditioning that might be kicking off or on historical traumas that might be being projected. Check your boundaries are coming from a loving place.*
>
> *The first few times you apply this, it may take two or three moments (or longer), but with practice, you'll be able to answer all those questions within one mindful pause.*

Reality checks

Let's end on a realistic note, because with romance, many of us are vulnerable to magical thinking and fantasy... I can't prescribe healthy romance for you; I don't know you well enough to allow for the nuances. What I have done here is to offer you the tools to

Chapter Five: ROMANTIC RELATIONSHIPS

support your journey in choosing and keeping healthy romantic relationships.

Dr John Gottman, who founded the Gottman Institute with his wife Julie Gottman, is famous for conducting 50 years' worth of research on how to maintain a stable marriage. The research showed that 69 per cent of problems in a relationship are, in fact, unsolvable (I am sure you understand why I am telling you this now, and not at the start of this chapter!). His research found that the number one predictor of divorce in the first six years of marriage is contempt. He says you don't need to know much else about a couple; if the people in the relationship are treating each other with contempt, the relationship is in trouble. All the tools offered here support you to manage differences rather than eradicate them; they help you to be kind to each other and develop empathy and understanding so that contempt does not have space to build up. They all focus on the relationship dynamic rather than advocating for an individual over the other.

The fact is, knowing all this means you can **start to** free yourself from the cycles of trying to change the people you date, or marry, and focus on choosing the right people for yourself and building new ways to love each other. I say 'start to' on purpose because this work has to become a practise and an approach rather than a final resolution.

Summary:

1. *Romantic relationships are important to us because of our biological need to keep the species alive.*
2. *Being aware of what ego state is being activated supports healthy intimacy and communication.*
3. *It is possible for you to change who you are attracted to... I did.*
4. *Seek further support for sex and love addiction if you relate to that section.*
5. *Red flags are warnings, yellow flags can be worked on, and green flags are to be appreciated.*
6. *There is no secret to healthy romantic relationships, but if you are willing to change and commit to finding healthy ways to communicate and manage conflict, you have the power to make choices that lead to romantic relational health.*

Chapter Six:
WORKPLACE RELATIONSHIPS

Reflective Question: 'Why did you choose the work you chose?'

Healthy workplace relationships have the power to change your daily life experience for the better. Negative experiences can leave as much of a mark as any other type of relationship trauma. When I was researching for this chapter, I scoured the internet for accessible reads offering information about the psychology of workplace relationships and the impact they have on us. Most that I came across fell into two categories. Either they offered ideas on how to be more successful, less anxious, more mindful, what to think, and how to speak to people in order for us to accomplish more power in our working lives. Or they were extremely academic and inaccessible to the general public.

I was able to find and read research articles about the relational dynamics of leadership and the importance of relationships in professional life (see Further Reading: Scandura & Meuser, 2000), and elsewhere made it clear that there is enough qualitative evidence to demonstrate that workplace relationships are considered an area of interest (see Further Reading: Gersick et al., 2000). It's an area of interest because we need to be able to make good decisions alongside our work colleagues, and in organisational set-ups they are also the people who will be reviewing us and will have an impact on our pay and promotional opportunities. But the articles I have just mentioned still focused on career mobility, not the impact our workplace relationships can have and what made us choose them.

I found a systemic review on workplace bullying which confirmed the already established link between victimisation and mental health. The researchers of this review went on to say that there is still not enough high-quality, longitudinal research being undertaken to really give us a solid idea of the negative effect of workplace bullying on people, or what makes people vulnerable to negative experiences in the first place (see Further Reading, Leach et al., 2003).

It was all very interesting, but not exactly what I was looking for. I couldn't find an accessible book or article which focused explicitly on relationship dynamics in the workplace. There was, however, an article about the impact of humour on workplace relationships (Further Reading; Kim and Plester, 2014), and I discovered that Gary Chapman has adjusted his five 'love languages' to fit workplace relationships in his book *The 5 Languages of Appreciation in the Workplace* (see Further Reading), which would certainly be a helpful follow-up read from what I've included here.

I wondered if the lack of accessible information, as you'll learn, is because, like other relationships, many of our work-based bonds are impacted by our histories and social lives. Do we just bring what we already know about relationships into the workplace? And how does this sit with business models that are financially driven? What about performers and musicians? Teachers? What about the self-employed?

Maybe the assumption is that the self-help books on other types of relationships will cover workplace relationships too… But I'll let you read the rest of this chapter so you can reach your own conclusion as to whether more information is needed to support healthy relationships in your specific work environment.

WHY WE CHOOSE THE WORK WE CHOOSE

It's not unusual for people to end up in careers that reflect something significant in their history. Sometimes it's the subject matter, sometimes it's the set-up, and sometimes it's the people. Most of us remain unconscious as to the choices that got us there – until something happens that means we want it to change, whereupon we start asking ourselves, 'Why did I choose this?'.

In his book *Willful*, Richard Robb discusses the idea that we tend to pursue outcomes that best satisfy our pre-existing desires and that not all our choices are rational. I feel like this hit the nail on the head for me in terms of what I have to offer you here.

Unlike lots of the research cited above, the information in this book is not going to act as guidance on how to answer interview questions like, 'Why do you want to work here?', and I don't think it's going to help you get your dream job or the promotion you've been denied. It's going to help you understand on a deeper level how your attachment styles have led you down the relational path you've chosen, and support you to solve any quandaries about why you chose the work you chose. You may be able to use what you learn about yourself to support your career mobility, but that, for me, will be a secondary gain.

Some of us have a very clear top level idea about why we chose our work. Maybe you're a teacher and you've always had a passion for helping children and young people, or maybe you have strong feelings about climate change and the only thing that made sense for you as a career choice was to work for a climate change charity. Or maybe your parents dictated the job you went into, and you didn't feel you really had any other choice. But beneath these seemingly rational choices, there is more to know.

Our workplaces and the relationships within them, can represent something very specific to us. For example: something from your schooldays, such as being accepted and feeling like you 'fit in'. Your colleagues might represent stability and co-operation, or maybe teams of people remind you of the risks you've taken in the past in order to feel accepted. If you work alone, work may represent a creative safe place, or a place of solitude that you like or don't like. Often, simply having the insight into what work or the people at work represent to you, and the emotions they evoke can help change how you approach certain things, if you want to.

Not always, but often, we follow a route that feels familiar. My mum was a singer and TV presenter and retrained as a counsellor in her fifties. I was a dancer and choreographer and I retrained in psychology in my twenties. So I chose something familiar. A similar thing happens in a less obvious way when we pick jobs that reflect our experiences and roles in our family – for example, someone who had to caretake a family member may be drawn to nursing, nannying or another helping profession.

Many of my clients who are in the public eye are people who only felt seen in their family and were affirmed for being the best and

Chapter Six: WORKPLACE RELATIONSHIPS

coming first at things throughout their lives. They ended up in careers that made them famous and allowed them to have an audience who could carry forward the affirmation for their talents. Someone who felt trapped, poor and powerless may compensate through being drawn to a high-pressured, high-earning job that allows them to feel powerful and free themselves from their childhood experience. Or the same person might go the other way and approach work with what we call a *lack mentality*, meaning they repeat their powerlessness, recreate the trapped feeling and never free themselves from the financial worry that plagued their childhood (see Further Reading: *Scarcity Brain*).

There's a phrase: *how you do one thing is how you do everything*. This means that you create and engage with similar patterns, people and dynamics in most aspects of your life, including at work. You may have started to notice this in yourself already.

On what might seem like the flip side but is actually a consistent pattern – if it keeps popping up for you, comparable to friendships and romance – your workplace relationships can allow you to access parts of yourself and ways that you don't feel are permitted elsewhere.

This means that, if you've done the majority of the hard work in previous chapters, this chapter will be more about fine tuning and applying what you've learned to the context of workplace relationships.

Exercise: Work Relationships Assessment

Take a moment to answer the following questions:
- *How do you feel about your workplace?*
- *How do you feel about the people you work with?*
- *How much of your stress and anxiety is related to work?*
- *Do you have career goals?*
- *Do you believe you can achieve your career goals?*
- *Do the feelings you have relate to work itself, the money you're paid, or the people there with you?*
- *Do you feel that your relationship to work impacts your relationships outside work?*
- *Do you want it to be different?*
- *How?*

WORK/LIFE BALANCE

When people come to therapy to help manage their workplace stress, I hear the term 'work/life balance' a lot. 'I've got no work/life balance', 'I need a better work/life balance', 'I don't seem to be able to find any work/life balance'.

Just for info: The term, work/life balance first appeared in the 1980s in conjunction with the Women's Liberation Movement. It was originally a phrase focused on making schedules more flexible and popularising maternity leave for child-bearing people. But the idea that working hours should be restricted, particularly for women and children, dates back to the 19th century (see Further Reading, Raja & Stein, 2014).

These days we use the term to describe the balance in how we prioritise the different parts of our lives and this balance is so important that people often seek out external support to make it happen. When I'm supporting someone to navigate their relationship with work some of the therapeutic questions I might offer are:

Are you relying on work to keep you busy to avoid your aloneness? Do you need workplace affirmation to bolster your self-esteem? Do you place more importance on workplace relationships than on other types of relationships? Are you trying to get others to recognise an unmet childhood need or want, via the work you do?

Rebalancing your work/life situation
There are two ways to rebalance your work/life situation. The first way is to take action at surface level and involves doing the practical things you need to do, to feel more balanced and comfortable in relation to work by re-prioritising the areas of your life.

An easy way to do this is to use a diary and diarise everything with different colours. Put 'work' in green, 'social life' in blue, 'family' in pink and 'personal' in yellow (pick your own colours and categories). Make sure you are comfortable with the balance between the different colours when you're done. On a weekly basis you want to feel content that you have enough of each category in your life – and it's also perfectly normal to have some weeks where it's mostly work and other weeks where it's mostly social; just the overall balance needs to feel satisfying to you.

Chapter Six: WORKPLACE RELATIONSHIPS

If you're unsatisfied or you feel stress kicking in when you look at your diary, make the necessary changes like organising an extra social event, cancel that fifth gym class, make space for some downtime, book in or move an extra client meeting. Commit to these changes. **Take it further:** what you notice about your reaction to these changes might help you further answer some of the questions listed above.

The second way to rebalance your work/life situation works on a deeper level. Do the internal work first. Dig deep by self-reflecting or through speaking to a therapist about what drives the imbalance in your work/life, lots of which I hope you will uncover throughout the rest of this chapter. Quite often we have to do this internal part first, in order to make the practicalities suggested above feel sustainable.

DIGGING DEEPER: THE WORKPLACE SYSTEM

When I refer to the workplace system, I am not referring to policies and bureaucratic processes. I am talking about the system that the people and relationships create in a workplace: a people system, a relational system.

Over the years I've spoken to enough employees and leadership teams, mostly through my consulting work and speaking engagements, to know that most workplace issues are relational and systemic and therefore need to be tackled from the top down.

The situation is different for those who work for themselves: therapists, performers, writers and digital creators, for example. These people experience things slightly differently as they are not functioning within a system that is already set in place when they arrive on the job; they move their own 'system' from working relationship to relationship (or contract to contract) – which has its own positives and negatives.

Regardless, when people ask me for help with a workplace relationship issue, I am consistently struck by the lack of knowledge between an individual's emotional wellbeing and the systemic nature of working with other people, whether you work with them for a day, a month or for ten years.

A good example: when an employee's mental health is declining, or they are burning out, it's often assumed they were simply overloaded at work or 'doing too much'. Maybe they were, but the sense that you are exhausted to the soul that accompanies what most of us call burnout can stem from how what's happening in the workplace system is being received, rather than from the workload itself.

Cast your mind back to our family chapter, where we looked at the family system and all the different roles it takes for the system to function, as well as the fact that most issues start with the parents (pp. 50-51). In our workplace relationships, because of the differences between people in age and experience, we can tend to bring with us our ***internal family system***, as well as other relationships, including friendships, romance and previous workplace experiences. When you look around an office full of people and visualise each person with their own relational history unconsciously following them around, you understand why workplace dynamics can deeply affect us.

Often, workplace issues are assigned to one group or another. A bit like when we were talking about family relationships. The children or sibling group can be the ones who are identified as having an 'issue', but usually it's a reflection of the parents, or in the case of a workplace system, those who represent parents. Because we are attracted to what we know, it is likely that – regardless of our occupation – our reaction to the relational system within the job is reflective of our past, or at the very least, the way we respond to the relational system comes from our personal history.

For example, if you find yourself rebelling against workplace systems, people or otherwise, it's likely you have some issues with the original system you came from – your family system – maybe you've always been keen to do things your own way and push back against authority or you find yourself activated into a fawn response in the workplace.

This can be true in all sorts of work environments. I once worked on a musical theatre show where the cast members were having anxiety and panic attacks, seemingly out of nowhere. While I was supporting them, I realised the issue seemed to relate to the constant changes being made within the cast and the crew. It left people feeling unsafe and out of control and as if they were not being valued or looked after. It was really my only option to do some damage control with the cast members by introducing skills to help them through their difficult feelings and understanding what was being activated inside them, but ideally I would have liked to have worked with the full crew to see what was happening for the people who held the power. Would they have kept changing things if they were aware of the impact on the performers?

The workplace 'family'
Some workplaces believe that family values are values that would benefit the workplace, though this assumes that everyone's family values will be about working together and supporting each other for the greater good, which is not always true. In a *Harvard Business Review* article, Joshua Luna (see Further Reading) writes about how bringing the word 'family' into the workplace can blur lines, exaggerate loyalty and create power dynamics where employees can be taken advantage of. All of which I have seen happen in real time.

As much as I think it's an attractive concept to have a 'work family', in practice, I really believe it is not good for our mental health, and it can actually lead to burnout rather than prevent it. The workplace needs to have workplace values and boundaries, not family values and boundaries. When you bring family values into the system, it triggers individual ideals of what their family was and what a family should be. Consequently, it can also trigger people-pleasing behaviours in line with people's need for belonging, fairness and reciprocation and, more unconsciously, for acceptance, approval and unconditional love – which the workplace is not responsible for. In other words, along with family values, you also get family issues.

I've worked with a handful of start-ups in various forms but my main role is usually to support the psychological wellbeing of the people involved as well as guide CEOs and CFOs on how to integrate good mental health into their brand.

One example in particular springs to mind. I worked with a company who in their first five years expanded from about ten employees to close to one hundred. They loved the idea of family values and it certainly drew people in. Everything was fine to start with, and this way of approaching their business seemed to cut it when the team was smaller, but as they hired more people from more varied backgrounds, the family values approach meant that boundaries were often crossed, and people were overworking, underperforming and pushing back in aggressive ways. Another boundary issue developed where people were using the workplace to process and share their private lives. Everyone knew far too much about everyone, and this resulted in all sorts of difficulties: communication glitches, micromanaging, resentment, envy, fear, lies, withholding, unfair salary increases and promotions, power play, difficulties in moving up the company, and more.

In this particular instance, I was brought in to work with two different teams in order to 'fix the issue on the ground', because people were clearly unhappy and often feeling burnt out. Unsurprisingly to me, it was the people at the top who were the main contributors to the dysfunction, because in lots of ways what was happening served them. They needed to understand how the expectations they were setting, and the behaviours they were modelling needed to change, if they really wanted things to improve.

As a CEO or a leader, it is upsetting to hear that it's what you are bringing into the workplace 'family' including your biases and control issues that are filtering down and provoking reactions in others. Having said that, we can't always hold the people at the top entirely accountable as the workplace is not a family and there will be other contributing factors that are disruptive to the system. It's usually the case that the entire system needs to adjust in order to be healthier – and often, people do not want to make those changes. This is mainly because it would mean making momentous modifications in how everyone uses the workplace, and most likely tolerating a lower quality of work and a drop in business in the short term whilst the system's focus realigns.

RELATIONAL BURNOUT

If you're feeling confused about the values you're expected to abide by and where your priorities should be, shame-based self-

Chapter Six: WORKPLACE RELATIONSHIPS

worth issues can surface, and people often simply work harder and become harsher on themselves in an attempt to look successful, productive and capable, while disguising a deeply held relational core belief that they are not good enough, this leads to what I call relational burnout.

GPs sign people off work every day in an attempt to make things better with the idea that giving patients respite from the workload itself will resolve the issue. However, I would argue that anyone who experiences relational burnout would benefit far more from reassessing their approach to the workplace (not the work itself) and the people within it. Maybe we could even start to separate types of burnout: burnout related to workload which is a practical issue and relational burnout, which is an internal, relational and shame-based issue.

I take it seriously because I've treated people who have been forced to stop working in order to quite literally save their own lives. I have even worked with someone who pushed themself so hard that they will be on hormone replacement therapy for the rest of their life, because of the stress their body and mind endured as a result of their behaviours in relation to work, in response to a lack of self-worth. The people I refer to here were highly successful, and they were most certainly responding to a sense of shame that runs far deeper than the impact of their workload.

How shame and burnout interact
Some of the most successful people on the planet have got to where they are via attempts to escape their personal sense of shame. Michael Jackson is a primary example. One of the most successful musicians of all time, he was clearly motivated and ambitious in his career and extraordinary at what he did, but he also quite literally burnt out when he died of cardiac arrest due to a lethal combination of sedatives and anaesthetic. He was addicted to these drugs, presumably for several reasons: to escape the traumas he had endured at the hands of his FOO and the resulting shame, to cope with his internal world plus a huge amount of responsibility, and to continue finding more power and greater successes, he worked himself to death.

You might look at MJ and think *how could shame be controlling his career to that extent? He was in the public eye almost every single day of his life – surely he did not feel ashamed of himself...*

Shame, particularly the type of shame that pushes people to do more than their nervous system can cope with, is a secretive emotion born out of damage done in relationships. It gets hidden, repressed and suppressed, and often leads to mental health issues like depression, anxiety and panic disorders that can appear to be related to work but often come to the surface when something about our relationships changes (for an in-depth look at how shame can affect your life, see *Healing the shame the binds you* in the Further Reading section).

We need healthy human interaction to maintain our mental health, it's like the oil that keeps the cogs turning. When we lack healthy human connection, it's much easier to overwork in response to shame because we lose the opportunity to 'check in' with others. We are more prone to making up stories in our minds about what other people think of us and trauma held in our bodies can resurface more easily.

Simone Biles, one of the greatest gymnasts of all time, surprised the world when she pulled out of the 2020 Olympic games because she knew her mental health was not where it needed to be. Gymnastics historically is a sport with a culture built on working towards burning the body and mind out and who ever can hack it the longest is considered the strongest. Although that has started to change during Biles's career after several abuse scandals, it took a lot of mental strength to protect herself like she did.

These particular games took place in Tokyo during the Covid-19 pandemic and were very different to what she was used to. Her family and support network were not able to be there to help her feel safe and provide the human interaction that supported her wellbeing. When she started struggling in her work, the observation from others, as quoted in the Netflix documentary *Simone Biles Rising* was that 'she was alone'. After she made the decision to leave the games, she says that shame consumed her, and she felt 'in jail with her brain and body'.

In her documentary, Biles explains that she worked through what was happening to her in therapy and describes in her own words how the trauma and shame held in her body from the sex-

Chapter Six: WORKPLACE RELATIONSHIPS

ual abuse she endured within the gymnastics world, on top her FOO trauma came to the surface during those 2020 games, she says her therapist suggested that if it hadn't have come up then it would have come up at another point in her career and, presumably had a similar or worse impact. In my professional opinion, it came to the surface for her during the pandemic because there was a lack of human contact. All the competitors had during those games was work. They had zero social connection to keep their psychological cogs oiled.

She protected herself from burning out by removing herself from the competition to do the internal work on the trauma and shame that surfaced. She re-aligned her priorities and focused on her relationship with herself and her husband and started to enjoy her work again, as evidenced through her success during the 2024 Olympic games.

For some people the shame that drives relational burnout appears to be correlated with a dynamic in a person's relationship with a caregiver or authority figure. They are trying to live up to the expectations of a powerful person and never feeling they ever quite get there. In the example of Michael Jackson, his father is known to have held a lot of power over him throughout his childhood and, like anyone who experienced this dynamic, he likely had a deeply held sense that he would simply never live up to, be good enough or supersede parental expectation. This creates shame that unconsciously pushes people to overwork and ultimately burnout.

On the flipside, some are disappointed, embarrassed or carrying shame from caregivers in their approach to work or lack of it. I am not her therapist but I know that in the case of Simone Biles, her birth mother had a substance abuse issue serious enough that Simone and her three siblings were all neglected and exposed to substances having priority in the family over anything else. Her and her sister were taken into foster care when they were young, ultimately to be adopted by her grandparents, who were her saving grace, but her experiences in infancy had a lasting impact.

People who carry their caregivers' shame, be that due to an addiction issue, lack of mentality, poverty, a lack of achievement or anything else, may find themselves trying to do things differently.

Unlike Simone's experience, without a healthy historic or current role model, they experience a sense of confusion and not quite knowing what is expected of them. They never feel that they meet the mark because they haven't witnessed someone else doing so. Preserving their mental health by preventing burnout doesn't feel like a choice they can make. I wonder if the latter is, in part, what happened with Micheal Jackson.

Preventing Relational Burnout
Working towards preventing relational burnout means making sure your self-worth is intact, and practising workplace boundaries that sustain it. Sometimes that means letting go of the gratification you get from others for working 'so much' or 'so hard', and for going 'above and beyond', as well as the *martyrdom* that can accompany the compulsive need to overwork. It means staying off the Drama Triangle (pp. 143-7) at work and re-teaching yourself that even when we are being paid to do something, our best is valuable enough and that we are all still learning along the way.

Here are some of the therapeutic questions *(pick the ones applicable to you)* that can help you understand why you personally might be prone to burnout in work relationships:

- What was going on inside of you at work that meant you couldn't stop what you were doing?
- Is it that you don't feel good enough around people at work?
- Is there a part of you seeking sympathy because you haven't had enough empathy elsewhere in life?
- Is there something specific that triggers you into letting work take over?
- Who taught you to undervalue yourself to the extent that you are sacrificing your own self-care and wellbeing in the face of perceived validation?
- What's the payoff?

You might answer these questions and gain some insight into what's going on for you relationally, and then decide that you would rather continue with what you are doing. Maybe the gratification and the martyrdom feels that good to you, or being on the

Drama Triangle is still working for you. That's fine by me, but I want it to be a choice that you can make and feel in control of, rather than a compulsive behaviour that takes control of your life and does more damage than good.

Work as an addiction

Although relational burnout and work addiction certainly crossover, they are slightly different things. In the previous section I connected burnout with a lack of self-worth in relation to ourselves and people at work. Work addiction can certainly be born out of that, but it can also relate to using work to change how we feel on a broader level too. For example, someone may overwork in response to a romantic relationship not going well, loneliness, a health scare, or a difficult relationship with themselves. Just as when we looked at sex and love addiction/avoidance, work addiction encompasses the other end of the spectrum – underworking to change how we feel, and yes, it is possible to burnout as a result of this. Either way, work is the thing you're using to escape your reality.

For many of us, work is a significant part of our adult lives, both in terms of our identity and how we are perceived. For some it provides a feeling of increased confidence, an opportunity to use skill and invest in passions for the good of others. It can be an opportunity to socialise and learn new things as well as to stabilise our income. We call these benefits ***positive reinforcers.***

When our relationship with work is unbalanced and we allow work to dominate our lives either through overworking or underworking, it's usually because there is something relational happening inside us that we want to avoid. We start to 'use' work to change how we feel. Just like any other process addiction (pp. 127-9) our patterns and rituals surrounding work may allow us to feel more in control of our emotions. Those emotions do not need to be positive. For example, we'd rather the stress of work than the stress of parenting or dating or exercising – these types of behaviours are known as negative reinforcers – the 'better the devil you know' type of thinking. What moves it into addiction territory is that it's having a detrimental effect on you or those around you.

There are lots of myths around work addiction (I've included a paper entitled 'Ten Myths about Work Addiction' in the Further Reading section if you'd like a deeper understanding). What I can tell you right now, though, is that work addiction is not about how many hours a week you work – it's about how you work and why you work. As the 'Ten Myths' article cited above points out, it feels obvious to correlate the word 'addiction' with time spent at work, but time is not a central piece of the diagnosis and under-working is very much a part of work addiction. You can work five hours a week and still have a work addiction if you are using it to change how you feel. Likewise, you can work a 60-hour week and not be addicted to work because you're still present and available for your other relationships and not using work to escape your reality. The symptoms of the addiction lie in the mental obsessions, rituals and efforts to feel differently about yourself.

Someone who puts things off and then overworks late into the evening might be motivated by avoiding having to be intimate with their partner or looking after their children or indeed avoiding their own loneliness, because these relational aspects are hard to predict and control. Work addiction can mean that work becomes your primary attachment and leaves little or no room for intimate relationships with yourself or others outside of work. Like any other addiction, only *you* really know if your relationship to work bears the hallmarks of an addiction.

As before, I am encouraging you to consider the addiction stance. Because the more you understand your work choices, your behaviour within your work relationships, and the impact your relationship with work has on your self-worth, the more choices you give yourself.

WORKPLACE BOUNDARIES

A 1960s social experiment by social psychologist Stanley Milgram took 40 male volunteers and assigned each of them the role of 'teacher'. The men were told that their job was to help a man, just like themselves, who was assigned the role of 'learner', to learn a list of word pairs. Every time someone made a mistake the 'teacher' was told to administer an electric shock. The experimenter told them to increase the shock level each time until a dangerous level of electric shocks were being given. In reality the 'learner' was actually Milgram's assistant; he didn't receive any shocks but pretended to be in pain when the shocks were administered.

What came out of this study surprised the researchers. The hypothesis had been that fewer than 1 per cent of the people involved would administer what they were told was a dangerous electric shock. But in fact 66 per cent of the 'teachers' obediently administered the highest level of shock despite believing the 'learner' was distressed and suffering a lot of pain. Milgram concluded that the 'teachers' had acted this way because they were pressured to do so by an authority figure and therefore could justify their actions by shifting responsibility of what was happening to the 'learner'. This experiment still stands as a great example of how people lose sight of their personal boundaries in the face of real or perceived authority.

Workplace boundaries can feel very different to boundaries in other relationships. Partly because we sometimes make work itself representative of an authority in our lives and on top of that we have actual authority figures to relate to. But, unlike authority figures from earlier in our lives such as parents or teachers many years older than us, these authority figures are, in reality, just other adults.

Another reason that work boundaries can feel different and are potentially more challenging is that we unconsciously apply an accuracy bias to the people or places we position as authority, as the men did in the experiment outlined above. This makes us more likely to convince ourselves that what a person in authority says, wants, does and believes is in some way superior to what we think and feel. Another reason is that, again, as above, many of us fall into an obedience mindset where we will do what we are told and pay less attention to our personal opinions and boundaries. The latter works for us because it means we have to use less brain power and we can rely on someone else to take responsibility for our actions: after all, we are just doing what we were told. This also gives us someone to jump on the Drama Triangle with, even if it's just within our own minds, if things don't go well. So, the payoff for not using workplace boundaries and deferring to someone else is that we give ourselves the choice to shift the responsibility, plus we don't have to cope with the difficult feelings and potential conflict that come up when we do use boundaries.

It could be said that having an accuracy bias, and following directions in spite of negative consequences, are both ways of attempting to secure approval from authority figures and/or to avoid responsibility. If you go back to your previous work on people pleasing (see pp. 73-5) you may be able to begin connecting the dots between the part of you who sought out love and approval in childhood and some of your difficulties with boundaries at work. Similarly, take a moment to think about how often responsibility is shifted around in your workplace system – is there a blame culture at play that encourages this? Can you see the Drama Triangle (pp. 143-7) playing out when no one wants to take responsibility for how they feel about something? I wonder how those men involved in Milgram's experiment felt about themselves when they were going home – believing they had agreed to do something that harmed another person. Were they really able to shift the blame, or was there a part of them that felt shame for what they had done?

Not using boundaries at work can have an additional impact on people around us too. Without them, we are less likely to be and feel assertive. If we don't use boundaries at work, we are likely to be less assertive. When we don't feel we can assert ourselves we feel resentful, envious, anxious, tired and angry more of the time, we are more likely to suffer burnout and the people who get to hear about it are often our family, friends and romantic partners; thus our other relationships can suffer. Said differently: when we displace the feelings we are left with, as a result of not using boundaries at work, we are at risk of shifting our relational work issues on to another type of relationship.

All this can take effect because when we meet with someone we perceive as an authority, we are unconsciously pulled into a less powerful place, one that reminds us of our childhood vulnerability. If you've done lots of inner child work, it may not affect you so much as you'll have a good sense of self-worth (hopefully) and you'll know when you are responding from a child ego state and how to stay in an adult ego state at work. But still – we were all

Chapter Six: WORKPLACE RELATIONSHIPS

children once, and we have all felt powerless, so at times we are all reminded of it. In addition, a toxic work environment will monopolise on a lack of boundaries with authority and likely create a Groupthink scenario (see p. 72) that is hard to challenge.

Conversely, in a healthy workplace, boundaries will be encouraged and respected and seen as a tool that supports us to provide the best quality of work we are capable of while maintaining our own psychological wellbeing.

Which category does your workplace fall into?

Setting boundaries at work

As you already know, boundaries are how intimacy is created and also what tells other people about how you want to be treated. So, let's look at the practicalities of setting boundaries within the workplace. I am going to avoid the basic *no work after 6pm* type of suggestion, because all jobs are different and it's not always applicable. Plus, as I explained in the section about preventing burnout, unless you've done the internal work, sticking to those types of practical changes isn't always possible.

The first thing to do is to take a bit of mental distance. Find a mental space where you can be more mindful and observant than you usually are at work. You could use the mindfulness exercise on p. 152 to help you get there. Start by observing your feelings in relation to work and the people in your workplace. Consider what these feelings mean about how you relate to people and how they impact your relationship within yourself. Do you value yourself as 'better than' or 'less than'?

The feelings you notice will indicate to you when a boundary is necessary. Anger or any variation of it (irritation, frustration, annoyance, passive aggression, and so on) is usually the main player. Fear may also be present. These emotions let you know that you need to implement something that helps contain and protect you and others at work. Usually, the feelings are not about the practical; they are about the way things are done or the expectations you perceive to be attached to them, and sometimes they will be about the system you are working in because it's triggering something from inside you.

Next, I want you to practise enquiring, as a way to gather information. Lots of people I've worked with don't know how to enquire at work without feeling scared, ashamed or angry. This comes from questions being shut down in childhood, most likely by authority figures (caregivers) who were angry, or fearful perhaps because they didn't know how to answer and that made them feel vulnerable. Similar things can happen in unhealthy adult relationships.

Remind your inner child it's healthy to ask questions and tell them you'll do it as a grown-up (see functional adult exercise on pp. 79-80), even if they are feeling scared. From your adult ego state, ask the person that has activated those feelings inside you what their thinking is. Phrase it gently by starting with a bit of gratitude, something like 'Thanks for bringing me on board and trusting me to get that done by end of day. I'd be grateful to know how urgent you think it is as I've got several other things that need to be completed today?'. The gratitude is important because, when said out loud or put in writing, it can help lower any anxiety that the request will be interpreted negatively.

Whatever the response you get, be it helpful or unhelpful, go back to your feelings and if anger, fear, anxiety or sadness are present in you as an adult, you need a boundary. But before you jump to respond and set an emotionally charged boundary, check in with your child self, in case they have taken it to mean something about them. Validate how they feel to take the charge out of the interaction. Use affirmations like the following: 'I know you feel sad when too much work is given to me, I want you to know I'll handle it and do my very best not to abandon me or you in the process'. Following this, you may feel empowered to set a verbal (or electronic) boundary with your authority figure by suggesting a different deadline – or it might be an internal boundary where you protect yourself by getting the work done in the kindest possible way you can.

To summarise: as a functional adult you can handle what's happening. And it's likely that the fear and upset that occurs within you is coming from a wounded child place. However, I'd add that of course you can feel all these things as an adult, not every single emotion or reaction stems from your childhood but the truth is that no one loses out when they support themselves internally.

Chapter Six: WORKPLACE RELATIONSHIPS

When you apply this stuff, you heal the parts of you that were not allowed to ask questions or have boundaries in childhood, the parts of you who were criticised or told off for doing things you didn't know were wrong. And, if you pay close enough attention, you might just discover more information coming from the unmet need and wants of your inner child about why you chose the work you chose.

Emotional dumping after work

A work related stressor that often occurs in relationships where two or more people cohabit – whether a romantic, family or platonic relationship – is that one partner has a stressful time at work and doesn't have or isn't using the tools to support themselves. They come home to perfectly content people and offload their resentment, anger, fear, sadness, anxiety and frustration; they then feel better, but the person on the receiving end of this 'dump' feels much worse and often won't be able to figure out why.

When you emotionally dump after work (although we do it about all sorts of things), you are effectively getting rid of the undesirable feelings you've carried home and are giving them to someone else to sort out. But they don't get sorted out because the other person is likely to withdraw or attack in response. They start to take on the emotions you haven't dealt with, usually initiating a Drama Triangle (pp. 143-7).

People emotionally dump because that's the dynamic they witnessed in their Family of Origin (FOO), where adults and/or authority figures did not take responsibility for their feelings and didn't have functional ways of talking about emotions or holding boundaries – so, taking your work stressors out on bystanders, may seem like a normal thing to do for you. You may even think that you are simply just telling the other person about your day. But if it is a one-sided monologue, where there is no interest in identification, solutions or feedback, you're not having a conversation, you're dumping.

It *is* important to have an outlet to talk about what's happening at work outside of work, especially if work's feeling difficult. But I want you to be aware of the differences between dumping your stress on someone else, or even simply talking things through with a friend or family member and then not addressing the issue at work. In the latter dynamic, you are in fact doing the opposite to the above – using your other relationships to avoid taking action at work and potentially avoiding intimacy in your other relationships too which will leave you feeling unfulfilled all round. You may be able to reframe things in your mind by talking about it, but reframing is hard to maintain if you refuse to address the issue head on.

Addressing the issue most likely takes the form of exploring what's going on internally and then using the most appropriate boundary for you at that time. Here are a few examples:

- Not working with a particular person
- Sticking to your time boundaries without exception
- Permitting yourself to have productive days and restful days
- Knowing your priorities
- Not taking work home with you, emotionally as well as practically
- Committing to staying off the Drama Triangle at work

If you are wondering whether you dump your work-related stress on those you see outside of work, seek some feedback. When you are in a humble enough space, ask a few people for honest feedback on their experience of relating to you and what they think could be different. Take on board the bits you can work with and leave behind the bits that you don't feel are relevant right now.

Resentment at work
The word 'resentment' originates from the French word 'ressentir' which effectively translates as 'to re-feel'. When we don't use boundaries most of us end up gathering lots of it. Often we use the word to describe an angry feeling but there's a difference between anger and resentment. Anger is contextual to the situation; it informs you that a boundary has been crossed, one that isn't always triggered from your history. When we talk about resentment, in any type of relationship we are talking about unprocessed anger which has developed into resentment over time.

Resentment is often layered with historical events that have not been worked through. Therefore, when it comes up, our reactions may seem a bit out of line with what is truly happening. Brené Brown (see Further Reading) speculates that resentment is closer to the feeling of envy than to that of anger, which I can get on board with.

Envy is an emotion that comes up when someone else has something that we want, and won't or can't allow ourselves to have. I may be resentful that my colleague got the credit for something I felt I contributed to, but I may also be envious that they allow themselves to be more visible with ideas and efforts. So, my work isn't simply to work through my anger, it's to get more comfortable with being more visible.

Here's an example: My client is considered to be an outstanding member of her team. She is often invited on major projects and is given big responsibilities. She performs well all round, but finds herself anxious and panicky when working with one particular person.

When she works with this person, she feels that she isn't given enough information and that her ideas are often pushed aside only to then be reimagined, whereupon her colleague takes the credit. This leaves her feeling angry, demotivated and envious that someone else has the confidence to snap up the credit she feels should be hers.

Over time, because she hasn't been able to create boundaries in relation with this person, or in her wider team, her anger lingers. She moves from feeling anxious and panicky as an adult to feeling young, vulnerable and powerless within her workplace relationships, further contributing to her angry feelings and highlighting where her envy stems from. She's now in touch with the resentment that is driving her anxiety. When she explores the childhood feelings that are emerging, she realises she has never worked through the envy she felt towards her siblings for seemingly knowing better, while leaving her to be scapegoated for negative things. On top of this, her expectations of the adults around her were not met, as they did not see her truth.

Unpicking a resentment like this provides helpful information as to how you choose to navigate any similar situations going forwards.

> *Exercise: Resentment and Envy*
>
> Write down or think of three things you resent in your workplace. For each one, identify what you are envious of, consider what it is that you feel you don't or can't have.
>
> Reflect on whether you could start to meet the want or need by changing something that is within your control.

MIXING WORK AND PLEASURE

Since we spend so much time in the workplace, it's likely we'll meet people along the way who become our friends and people we may become romantically involved with. As this is a book about relationships, I felt the need to include a section on how these relationships crossover.

There is some evidence that people who integrate work with non-work-related activities – in other words, friends and romance – have a lower sense of wellbeing because there is no official downtime; there are always workplace stimuli around. All of the information and guidance in this book's friendship and romance chapters apply when this crossover happens, even more prominently when you are involved with someone sexually or romantically at work as your work/life balance can start to wane.

In addition, the lack of separation can negatively impact your other workplace relationships. If you are close friends with a work colleague it may feel hard not to favour them, even if their skills are not what you need at that time, which can lead to a lower quality of work and invite criticism from others. It can also lead to you having to take responsibility for a comparably increased workload than if you'd worked with someone more capable than your friend. Friendships at work between people at different levels within a team or company can also cause issues unless agreed boundaries are adhered to, which we tend not to do within friendships in the same way we do workplace or romantic relationships. This is less of an issue if you most often work for yourself, by yourself – but the essence still stands.

If you are romantically or sexually involved with a colleague,

Chapter Six: WORKPLACE RELATIONSHIPS

you may notice that it is harder to concentrate because the object of your affection is so close by. And, if things go wrong, the negative impact doesn't only affect one or some areas of your relationships, but most of them, including your performance at work. And dare I mention that the breakdown of sexual relationships in the workplace, where one person feels they have been taken advantage of or wronged, can lead to accusations that can affect your reputation.

There are positives to mixing work and pleasure, however. Lots of people do better at work when they are more deeply acquainted with their colleagues, they have more empathy and understanding, and are more likely to support each other appropriately. In addition, wonderful romantic relationships can be born out of getting to know each other in the workplace first, as you can learn a lot about a person from how they behave at work – things you may not find out until much later if you dated them outside of work. So, if your close friends and lovers are also at work with you then so be it.

Therapeutically, here are the questions I'd ask you to reflect on when mixing work and pleasure:

- What effect is this having on me?
- What effect is this having on my family?
- What effect is this having on my sexual and romantic relationship(s)?
- What effect is this having on my other workplace relationships?
- Am I repeating anything from my history?
- Are there any red flags I am ignoring due to the blurring of boundaries?
- Am I able to distinguish between personal and workplace-related matters?

If your response to these questions is a mostly positive response then great – keep doing what you're doing and make sure to notice if your self-worth dwindles at any point. If your response to these questions is mostly negative, please consider these additional questions:

- Why would I continue relating to people like this?
- How am I feeling about myself?
- What boundaries do I need to work on?
- Is there someone I know who could help me troubleshoot what's going on?

Returning to why you choose the work you choose...
Let's return to our initial reflective question, *'Why did you choose the work you chose?'*

With all the information you've gathered through the reading in this chapter, are you now closer to answering it for yourself? Is it about the people? The work? The workplace? Or is it more to do controlling and changing how you feel internally?

Your answer may change over time, as may your perspective, and that's perfectly normal. This work is all about creating a window of opportunity for you to make healthier and happier choices whilst reserving the right to change your mind at any point.

Summary

1. *Where we work is not an accident – on some level we have chosen it.*
2. *Burnout is often driven by a shame-based core belief system.*
3. *The work system you're part of may remind you of your original family system or groups you have been part of, historically.*
4. *When emotions run high at work and you don't face them, it can affect your other relationships too.*
5. *Mixing work and pleasure has both its positives and its negatives.*

Chapter Seven:
ONLINE AND DIGITAL RELATIONSHIPS

Reflective Question – 'Are you in a relationship with a person or an algorithm?'

I am writing this almost exactly four years to the day since our relationships with our families, friends, romantic partners (for those living apart) and our colleagues all moved online – or at least became more digitally based than they ever had been before. In 2020, the pandemic hit and the world went into lockdown.

We all responded differently. For some, the change was devastating, and for others a relief. Either way, everyone lost something in terms of in-person relationships, and as digital relationships started to adopt a greater presence in our lives, we all had to find ways to adjust.

I use this as a starting point because, like many of us, and despite supporting people to navigate in-person relationships for many years, I only sincerely started to think about online and digital relationships when it became my only option.

During this period, I did some work with a well-known computer software company to help promote the idea of digital health. I liked this concept because all my work so far had been about mental/emotional health, physical health or relational health, and there were very few norms or even guidelines around what we could call digital health even meant. The campaign I was involved in was aimed at making online and digital relationships possible and healthy at all ages. In this chapter, I'm going to share some of the work we did and expand it into the world of relationships.

One of the primary things I learned, while researching for my role and moving my entire therapy practice into a virtual world, was that online and digital relationships have been around for far longer than people like me, who prioritise in-person relationships, might realise. I also recognised that without the internet,

our in-person relationships would look remarkably different.
With this in mind, there are two focal points in this chapter. Firstly, there is the relationship with the software that enables you to have digital relationships. Secondly, there are the practicalities of creating and maintaining this type of relationship and where your mental health sits within it all.

DEFINING ONLINE AND DIGITAL RELATIONSHIPS

Let's define an online relationship as a relationship (see definition of relationship on pp. 10-11) between people who have met online and who know each other mainly via the internet or an app, in various forms like text messages, phone calls, video calls, gaming, chatrooms, or via a virtual character such as an avatar. This type of relationship may not *always* take a digital form, it may constitute just one part of the relationship. The relationship can be with a family member, friend, romantic partner, sexual partner, colleague, client, gaming partner, or artificial intelligence.

There is the type of online relationship that starts and stays online, the type where you stay connected with an old friend exclusively through the internet, and the type where you start out online and then forge an in-person relationship.

I would argue that lots of our relationships are already a hybrid of in-person and online. Think about how many days in a week you text your closest friend versus how many times you see them in person. You probably text them more often than you see them; therefore you are maintaining your relationship online. So, depending on your personal definition of an online relationship, even if you don't think you have any exclusively online relationships to explore, you will still gain from this final chapter.

THE PROS AND CONS OF ONLINE RELATIONSHIPS

With the other types of relationship in this book, with the exception of the section on mixing work and pleasure, I haven't taken much time to consider the pros and cons, mainly because the psychological pros of being in healthy relationships will always outweigh the cons. But our online relationships are little

Chapter Seven: ONLINE AND DIGITAL RELATIONSHIPS

different. Social media relationships, for example, do not hold all the same benefits as an in-person relationship. It's nice to be able to see what people are up to, and to potentially connect with like-minded people, but comparatively speaking, you're offered far less information than you'd get in person. It's interesting to consider the pros and cons and how online relationships impact us and our wellbeing, so that you can make a choice about how you engage with them.

One of the pros of online relationships is that they can be great for our self-esteem. Dating and friendship apps allow people to explore their own likeability and desirability without taking the emotional risks of rejection and consequent hits to their self-esteem that would be present if they did the same thing in person. The opposing con, though, is that if someone doesn't have a solid sense of self-worth and doesn't know how to work on their self-esteem, they may interpret unsuccessful online connections to mean they are not likeable or desirable – and, at the same time, try to use their interactions to compensate for self-esteem, which in turn can lead to a decline in their all-round mental health.

The main risk to our mental health with digital and online relationships is that we don't have to feel the uncomfortable and intimate emotions that we experience if we were saying and doing the same things in person. This means we don't get the opportunity to practise circumnavigating the appropriate emotions to the degree we would in person. Consequently, our window of tolerance isn't being stimulated in the same way, which ultimately means we may take longer to become aware or indeed bypass entirely much of the self-awareness that supports healthy intimacy. Having said that, you could also position this as an opportunity to practise saying and doing the things – for example, like setting boundaries – which you find difficult or even impossible in person. So, in terms of pros and cons for your mental health, I guess it depends how consciously you are using online relationships.

Because of the above, online relationships are intimate in a different way to in-person connections (I expand on online intimacy on page 203). Some people feel more comfortable sharing intimate details about themselves digitally, because they don't have to experience the same level of uncomfortable feelings, it doesn't impact their social arousal levels quite as much, and that can be very helpful. I am aware that working with a therapist online can feel much easier in some ways (if harder in others) for this very reason. The con is that we are also left to create stories in our own mind about the person we are communicating with, be that an online friend, therapist or other. And some say that the likes of therapy apps encourage our minds to translate even the more intimate relationships into a game, with no commitment or responsibility that you can pick up and drop at any time (see *Algorithmic Intimacy* in Further Reading).

If we never meet someone in person, we never get a true sense of the other person's physical energy, and we are at risk of creating an inaccurate idea of who they are. The image we create is more a reflection of our own fears and desires than a realistic idea of who the other person is. Hence, your perception of what's happening is based only on your own reactions, which means the relationship is mainly about you and your relationship with yourself. This may contribute to narcissistic traits and a lack of experience in navigating intimate interpersonal relationships in real life.

In online therapeutic relationships, this is not so much of an issue as it's the kind of thing we work through, but in other types of online relationships these projections can have a detrimental effect on our wellbeing. It is also why, when I offer online therapy sessions, I am constantly asking people about what is happening in their body, far more than I do if I am with them in person. In person, I can see what's happening, I can feel their energy more accurately and I can pick up on things like mirroring between the two of us, which means that it's easier to work with what therapists call the **counter-transference**, a term that refers to the therapist's feelings about the client. It's an important part of being able to empathise and understand our clients more intimately. On a screen I can often only see the person's head and torso, so I need my client to do a bit more work around identifying what's happening in their body. Some people like this and some don't and it's an unlikely question to transfer into

Chapter Seven: ONLINE AND DIGITAL RELATIONSHIPS

any other kind of relationship. Although there will still be plenty of counter-transference happening, it's easier for both therapist and client to feel things less when working online.

Since the pandemic, it's workplace relationships that have probably changed the most. Nowadays many people can work from home, for at least a couple of days a week, if their profession allows it. Office-based roles that demand five days a week in the office are perceived as rigid and inflexible. Lots of people find that the pro of working digitally means they can avoid the interpersonal moments of the workday and they can be more productive with fewer interruptions. Equally, employees I worked with during this transition noted that working from home meant missing the in-person moments where ideas were shared casually and what I'd call *therapeutic strokes* from colleagues were not happening for them. Missing this can impact the individual's gravitas and movement through the company, as well as influence their impact in meetings and on their teams, not to mention how they feel about themselves at work.

Other pros in online relationships include: being able to get to know people before you meet them, which gives you an increased sense of control. It is a way of connecting with people who you already know have similar interests to you. If you are very busy but also keen to meet new people, doing this online can be very time efficient.

Other cons in online relationships include: it feels easier for the people you're communicating with to be dishonest with you which may affect your ability to trust in the longer-term. If your connections don't work out for you, it can be damaging to your mental health. You may also put yourself at risk of homophobia, racism, sizeism, ageism and other prejudices, depending on how you set up our profile because people are often disconnected from the comments they make about others online. Your identity is out there for the world to see or steal – fraudsters create fake, copied accounts often, and your online presence makes it more likely to happen to you. There is also evidence that as online dating has become more popular there has been an increase in the incidences of sexual violence.

You can read more about the pros and cons of online relationships, and make your own decisions about whether one outweighs the other, in the 'Benefits and Dangers of Online Dating Apps' study cited in the Further Reading section for this chapter.

> **Exercise: Personal pros and cons**
>
> There will be many more pros and cons to your online relationships that I haven't touched on here. I invite you to reflect on, or even make a list of, the online relationships you have and what they offer you, as well as what they lack...

ONLINE AND DIGITAL BOUNDARIES

Boundaries in this type of relationship are the limits you set for yourself based on the effect the pros and cons the relationship has on you. Like our boundaries in real life, our online boundaries are as unique as we are, and can change over time. My definition of boundaries remains the same as it is in all other scenarios: boundaries protect and contain you and other people; they define who you are and create intimacy.

Here are some examples:

You always have the right to decide if you want your information and/or image online. I've met people who have almost no online footprint – to be honest it was a bit of a red flag at the time because I couldn't look them up – but the reality is that I just had to get to know them the old-fashioned way and ask them questions in person. I found it thought-provoking that it was out of the ordinary for me that the person wasn't searchable – but that was their boundary and it told me a little bit more about who they are. You may decide that you want to be online for work but make nothing searchable that is personal, including your face. You may be the other way inclined and be very comfortable showing your face and your life on the internet. Whichever way you swing, though, it's important to be curious about other people's boundaries and to respect them during your online use.

Another example of a boundary is to set a time limit for your-

Chapter Seven: ONLINE AND DIGITAL RELATIONSHIPS

self. This could be that you permit yourself one hour a day communicating online, or maybe allow no online relationships after 7p.m., or choose to not check dating apps during work hours. You get to decide if that includes phone calls, emails, apps like WhatsApp, and text messages too.

You may have an online boundary around sharing photos of yourself in direct messaging conversations. Maybe you share your face with someone you are communicating with, but not your body. Maybe you share certain parts of your body, but not others.

Some other online and digital boundaries to consider are:

- The age and location of the people you connect with
- How many people you are in conversation with at any one time
- The level of sexuality you are willing to share
- The amount of time spent communicating before you meet them in real life
- Treating and speaking to others the same way you would if you were with them in person
- A commitment to not ghosting people
- Enabling or disabling notifications
- Not comparing your life with what you see online
- Turning off blue ticks and seen stamps

> **Exercise: Online Boundaries, step by step, adapted from pp. 39-42**
>
> Boundaries are how we tell people about ourselves, and that is never more important than when we communicate with people online. Because there is no opportunity for the other person to pick up on our physical energy, we have to actively build their knowledge about us by telling them where our limits are.
>
> **Identify the boundary that you want to create and maintain**
> You can use the suggestions above to get you started.
>
> **Before you say or type it, imagine yourself using the boundary**
> Think about how you would use it offline as well as online and

see if it feels different. Practise alone and at a pace that works for you, as a warm-up, so to speak.

Set the boundary
Once you feel comfortable with what you've practised, set the boundary with the relevant person/people/thing.

Feel the feelings
As discussed, with online boundaries we sometimes feel less of an emotional charge compared to using boundaries in person, but it remains important that you feel your emotional reaction to what you've said. It's the feelings you feel that give you feedback about yourself and help you understand what you need out of online relationships, going forwards.

Repeat as necessary.

MIXING ONLINE AND IN-PERSON RELATIONSHIPS

For some people, crossing the boundaries from communicating online to meeting in person represents behaviour that is, at best, not the norm, and at worst, dangerous, which has been as evidenced by the rise in sexual violence linked with online dating. However, when I asked my social media followers what their experiences were, the majority had positive things to say (and the irony of turning to my social media followers for insight for this chapter is not lost on me!). A few had fallen in love, some had met great friends and others had connected with work opportunities that served them well. There are, of course, lots of stories about meet-ups that didn't go so well, but as it becomes more and more 'normal' to meet people after communicating with them online, I think we will all become much more attuned to the pros and cons of mixing in-person and online relationships, if that isn't happening already.

The role of fantasy in online relationships
A complication that I don't see talked about so often, is that our

Chapter Seven: ONLINE AND DIGITAL RELATIONSHIPS

online relationships leave space for us to engage in a fantasy which can feel nice but can also set us up for unrealistic expectations. Our unconscious expectations are often made horribly conscious when we meet with someone we thought was going to be 'perfect' in inverted commas, because **perfect isn't a thing, it's an illusion essentially made up by an amalgamation of the things that you have loved or lacked in your life so far.** Be it a friend, date, estranged family member or person in a workplace relationship, we all do it. We all project the care we want and need on to others and although we do it in other types of relationships, online connections are probably the easiest place for fantasy to run its course. In addition, whilst we are communicating online and involved in fantasy, we tend to imagine ourselves as emotionally 'safe', because we can shut down the communication if we need to. In effect, the fantasy doesn't have to become real.

Fantasising is a great way to experiment with ideas that in real life you'd never actually go through with. The easiest example is sexual fantasies. Lots of people have sexual fantasies about being either submissive or dominant (amongst other things), but in reality, acting them out would feel scary, awkward and potentially put someone at risk. Online relationships allow us to engage with fantasy in a way other relationships do not, and it is easier to stop things going too far if you catch them early enough.

If the other person starts showing early signs of being inappropriate, or scaring you or becoming abusive, you can block, report and move on without too many negative consequences. In person, shutting down an encounter or a conversation is far harder, can feel scary and potentially create even more risk with the wrong type of person. I know I am not alone when I reflect on some of the people I met up with during my online dating career and get a shiver of fear down my spine about what could have gone wrong. What got me into that pickle? Three things, actually. First, I wasn't listening to what my nervous system was telling me; second, I hadn't thought about what my boundaries were going to look like in this type of relationship; and third, confusing my fantasy about who the person could be with what I realistically felt okay with.

An example comes to mind – *and when you read this you may think that I must have been completely out of my mind to do it, but,* as for many young people seeking romantic and sexual companionship, up to a point this didn't feel odd at all – until it did. I was got chatting to a guy I had been matched with on a dating app and then we started sending voice notes to each other which, in true millennial fashion, freaked me out at first. But then the therapist in me decided it was better than just texting, because I could hear the other person's voice and the tone of what they were saying. We agreed to meet up. He gave me an address which when I arrived, turned out to be the car park of a car dealership (!?). That was a bit strange, but the next thing that happened was that he invited me into his car, and I got in (!!!). Already you can see that this situation was hard for me to shut down in real life, and I didn't know this person well enough to sense what would happen if I said 'no'. He then drove around, and we chatted, and we ended up going for a meal, where I soon realised he was probably high on marijuana and quite a paranoid person. This was demonstrated when he showed me all the security cameras set up in his home and quizzed me on what my Myers-Briggs personality type was. So, did I find a way to leave? Nope – I sat there, eating a meal I wasn't enjoying, and becoming more and more spooked and then... got back in his car (!!!!!!!). It was only when we were getting closer to where my car was that I started to pray that he wasn't going to continue driving past my car and not let me out. My heart started beating really fast, and I had to control my breathing in order to appear calm. To my total relief, I got back in my car, drove home and never spoke to him again. A great example of where my online communication, and the fantasy and expectations I'd created, did not serve me so well.

Conversely, I have also had positive experiences. I met my now husband on an online dating website and it's safe to say that went well. I'd add, however, that I think it turned out well because we stayed online and in-person friends for the first two or three years and got to know each other before we embarked on any type of flirting or physical contact. So... how can we help ourselves assess our ideas and fantasies about the person we are communicating with, and decide who is safe to meet up with and who is not?

I have some difficulty in answering this because I can't possibly predict every person who is safe and not safe for you, without

Chapter Seven: ONLINE AND DIGITAL RELATIONSHIPS

knowing you personally – and I don't know what your fantasies about the people you meet with are likely to be. What I can offer, though, are some warning signs to look out for within your online communications. Unlike in previous chapters, most of these are about what you observe in the other person which should make them tangible enough to apply.

Warning signs in online relationships

- No profile photo – This one always gets a thumbs down from me.
- You're immediately in a fantasy world about them – This probably means they haven't given you enough information about themselves, so your mind is making up things to fill in the gaps early on.
- They won't send photos – Although too many photos too soon can feel a bit over-eager, no photos at all may also be a little suspicious.
- There are long gaps between their responses – I hesitate to judge this one too quickly but it can indicate a lack of investment or that their focus is elsewhere.
- They ask you for money – Big no.
- The say they are falling in love with you before you've met – This indicates they are involved in a fantasy of you, not who you really are.
- They 'warn' you – If someone feels the need to warn you about themselves, listen to them.
- They tell you too much about their other relationships – This might indicate that they are using conversations with people online to process other relationships, rather than authentically connecting with new people.

It's not to say you shouldn't meet with someone who demonstrates these warning signs, but you might want to tell someone else where you are and have a strong get-out plan. In fact, I'd recommend planning both these options anytime you meet up in person with someone from online; it'll help you feel safer. Using the mantra 'I can leave at any time' can also be helpful, it empowers you to stay connected with yourself and know if you need to get yourself out of an encounter. And that feeling,

I could argue, is the biggest warning sign of all. That sense that you are unsafe is communicated when your nervous system goes into a stress response and starts telling you to fight, flight or freeze.

In addition to the above warning signs, I'd advise against getting in the cars of people you know nothing about! Do your first meet-up in a public coffee shop. The first meet should just be you making sure they are who they say they are. If everything aligns, and if you like them, then you can organise more meet-ups in less public places, if you want to, and eventually, after you've got to know them a bit and you've dropped any major fantasies about who they could be to you, that's the time to think about spending time alone with them. Naturally, fantasies about who the other person is, or is not, can survive a long time into any type of relationship, something that can help is to keep checking in with yourself about what real time evidence you have about who the person is.

Exercise: Fantasy detox

Consider a 'fantasy detox' if you answer yes to one or more of the following questions:

- Have you ever lost time fantasising about someone you've met online?
- Do you find yourself distracted by the fantasy of someone you've met online?
- Do you find yourself in online wormholes about people you've met online?
- Have you ever stayed connected with someone online rather than going to sleep when you are tired?

The detox
- What is the number one thing you would like to change in your online relationships?
- Why do you want that to change?
- What are three things you like to do that do not require any

> online involvement? (This can be as simple as thinking about puppies or as active as cross stitching or exercising – it really doesn't matter as long as you are changing your focus. The mindfulness exercise on pages 152-3 will also help with this.)
>
> For one full day, make a note each time you find yourself fantasising about someone you've met online (you can repeat this as often as you want).
> Engage in one of the three things you identified above instead of continuing with the fantasy.
> After the craving to be online passes (can take up to 30 minutes), ask yourself what triggered you to go into fantasy. Did you have an unwanted emotion you wanted to escape from? If you dig a little you may find out what purpose fantasy holds for you and therefore give yourself a choice as to whether you engage with it or not.
>
> **Take it Further**
> Commit to halting fantasy when it happens. Practise the 'three-second rule' which takes into consideration that we cannot control our first thoughts, but we can control our second thoughts and what we do with them. If you find yourself in fantasy, count 1, 2, 3 and change your focus – potentially to one of the three things you identified above, but any alternative will do.

Additionally I'd suggest avoiding alcohol and drugs for the first couple of meets. Even if you are meeting for physical intimacy, do it clean and sober so that you can keep your choices and boundaries in place. I am grateful that I was sober the evening I got into the car of a stranger. Things could have gone very differently, had I been drinking at the time. I know lots of people find sober intimacy, sex in particular, a bit scary but let's face it – scarier things can happen if you're hooking up with someone you've not vetted yet. If you can't bear the thought of sober hookups then maybe meeting with strangers on the internet for sex isn't for you right now, and it would be worth exploring what need or want you are trying to get met by putting yourself in that position.

YOUR RELATIONSHIP WITH THE ALGORITHM

Algorithms are a set of rules designed to solve specific issues. They are used within any application designed to match you with other people online. The bit we don't usually consider, unless we are having a negative experience with them, is our relationship to the algorithm itself.

I have, on several occasions, declared that 'the algorithm hates me' when my social media content doesn't get as much engagement as I would like. Within the rules of algorithms, generally, the more time you spend on the platform, the more positive reinforcement it'll offer you in the form of engagement, and so, the less time you spend on the platform the less it offers you. For this reason, if you are using online connections, and social media in particular, to help you feel more connected and better about yourself, an algorithm can become a punishing taskmaster that sets you up to obey it. In some ways, if you let it, it can become an authority figure in your life, one who tells you what to do and how to behave in relation to it – which is, at the very least, not the healthiest of relationship set-ups and, on some level, you may have a similar response to any other type of authority in your life (see pp. 177-181).

I have clients using dating apps who have given the algorithm a lot of power in their lives. Their response when things they post online don't get as much reach or attention as they would like is to feel frustrated and to believe it reflects something negative about themselves or their social network. People might say things like 'Does everyone hate me?' No, everyone does not hate you but when you don't get the attention you're trying to elicit, you are projecting your fears onto the algorithm.

Likewise using apps to connect with potential romantic or sexual partners and friends gives us the opportunity to narrow down our search using categories like age, gender, location and interests. And yet sometimes we are still presented with people who we don't find attractive or interesting. Clients of mine have wondered out loud what the algorithm is 'thinking' about them. They say, 'The app must think I am a lonely old spinster,' or 'I can't do dating apps anymore, no one I find on there is really looking to

Chapter Seven: ONLINE AND DIGITAL RELATIONSHIPS

settle down.' And when we hear ourselves say things like this, we start to realise that our online relationship is currently not with other people but with the algorithm, app, game or website itself. Fundamentally, most digital relationships leave us vulnerable to being used by the algorithms involved. To further my examples above, Facebook 'friends' and Instagram 'likes' are not really driven by friends and people who like you, but by self-developing algorithms targeting specific sets of people. Which means you are fundamentally in a relationship with artificial intelligence, not the people you are engaging with. You can, of course, as part of your digital health, take the time to really curate your feed by selecting who and what you want to see when you open your app, but mostly people choose not to do this and even if you do, you are still vulnerable to suggested accounts and adverts targeting the set of people the algorithm believes you fit into, even if you see yourself differently.

Even with our best efforts at play, algorithms are written to draw us in and be addictive. They can make you feel both great about yourself and knock you to the ground, and if this were an in-person relationship one could easily label it as abusive. We chase the highs by continuing to engage, hoping our fears will be diminished and our wishes will come true, and give away more and more data about ourselves, because it's addictive, but ultimately all we do is make the app developers richer.

Algorithms are, like most things, not all bad. In dating and friendship the very long process of getting to know if someone has the same interests, hobbies and values as you becomes a total breeze – because it's all written down in black and white on their profile. Is this shortcut a good thing for you? Or would you prefer to get to know someone more slowly? Have a think about it because if we hand ourselves over to an algorithm to suggest who we should connect with, we can allow ourselves to be led and used by artificial intelligence. Most people do not like the idea that they are being used or abused in any kind of relationship and as always awareness is key to making the relationship safe and healthy for you.

> *Exercise: Where's your relationship with the algorithm at?*
>
> Take a moment now to reflect on what you think the algorithm you come into contact with most often makes of you. What type of person do you think it thinks you are?

In summary, whether you've had a positive or negative experience of algorithms, all they do is respond to data we knowingly or unknowingly give them about ourselves and our lives. I have had experiences where I am convinced my phone can read my mind because I am getting adverts for something I've thought about doing or buying privately, as in I haven't said it out loud yet, but the truth is that algorithms can get really good at predicting our next steps. The moment I click through on a holiday ad I am inundated with holiday adverts, suggestions about swimsuits, luggage, hair removal devices, and of course further holiday ads and I'll be asking myself how on earth my phone knew I needed a new suitcase. What is shown to you reflects who you are and where you are right now, as well as where the algorithm predicts you are going.

To use this as an aid in your self-development journey, think about this: your response to what an algorithm presents you with may simply be highlighting how you feel about a part of your relationship with yourself. If we choose to become willing to use what algorithms show us about ourselves to develop more consciousness of our own and stay mindful of how we feel in response to what is reflected back to us, I think many of us would have some very interesting things to think about and work on.

ONLINE INTIMACY AND NON-VERBAL COMMUNICATION

Consciously or unconsciously, people often choose online relationships because they have experienced pain in their interpersonal relationships; there is often carried generational trauma or a lack of choice and opportunity available to them. A lack of choice might be due to their work situation; maybe they work alone so don't have a community available to them, or maybe bad luck in relationships and betrayal has led them towards a self-sufficient way of operating.

In therapy we sometimes break the word intimacy down to 'in-to-me-see' and it means, as a reminder, allowing yourself to be seen and seeing the other person for who you both are. This occurs through understanding where you end, and the other person starts – in other words, using and observing boundaries with love. Just like in our in-person relationships, authentic online intimacy feels vulnerable and it's how lasting connections are built. Those first few exchanges, as much as you might be total strangers, can tell you a lot and be the foundations to an intimate exchange. In fact, I was once told that a person will tell you all you need to know about themselves in the first seven minutes of meeting them, if you are willing to listen. Online relationships are no different. Your initial contact says more about the type of person you're communicating with than you might give it credit for. And sometimes what you're looking for is not in what they say, but in their non-verbal communication. Non-verbal communication online is specifically about pace, tone and timing, as you can't witness their body language and eye contact like you would in person.

Online there is less opportunity to witness non-verbal empathy cues that would usually occur face to face and support intimate relationships. In fact, in his book *Algorithmic Intimacy*, Anthony Elliott talks about how Tinder introduced an 'Are You Sure?' feature in 2021, to try and prevent people from sending potentially offensive messages that may come across as offensive and lack empathy and compassion.

The act of putting a screen between you and another person could also be considered non-verbal communication in itself. And it can be helpful. It provides the opportunity to skip over the bit about meeting new people, where your anxiety spikes, can be a great practice ground for anyone who feels they suffer with anxiety in social situations. There are even emerging treatments for anxiety that include virtual reality situations in which people can practise new social behaviours, while knowing they are in the safe hands of their therapist.

If you tend to feel that the anxiety involved in this kind of meeting far outweighs your desire for intimate relationships, then it can be valuable to practise new behaviours with a screen between you and the other person whether that relationship ends up staying online or not – as long as you stay aware of all we've talked about so far in this chapter, use your boundaries, look out for any warning signs and take them seriously.

A note on 'text speak' and emojis
Aside from missing out on our usual non-verbal cues, there is a lack of online intimacy when we use 'text speak', when we shorten words, miss out vowels, and so on. If you're too young to remember how this started, it was because when text messages first became a thing, we were restricted in how much we could write and how many we could send. Even though we can now write unlimited lengthy messages, there is a hangover. We still use shortened versions of words and abbreviations like TBH (to be honest), LMK (let me know), LOL (laugh out loud) and many more.

Emoticons, or emojis, were the mobile phone industry's answer to this. They are lots of fun but can be easily misinterpreted. If you go and get your phone now, have a look at your top five emojis. Mine are: 👍 (thumbs up) 😂 (laughing face with tears) 🙏 (gratitude hands) 🙈 (face peeking through fingers) and 🥳 (party face).

Interestingly, I feel very boring and old that those are my top five! How do you feel about yourself when you look at your top five emojis?

I am not going to break down each one of my top five, but let's just look at the 'thumbs up' emoji to start with. What does it mean to you? According to my phone, it could mean any variation of a positive response: okay, good, awesome, yes, and so on. But the trigger words for each emoji are always changing. Emoji selections are based on how people around you are using emojis, so if people started using the word 'cat' in conjunction with the emoji of a fish, you would also see that selection on your phone.

I use my 'thumbs up' emoji, most often, to communicate a positive response, but unless I explicitly clarify whether my positive reaction is simply an acknowledgment of what has been said or an agreement to be somewhere or do something, I leave room for misinterpretation. It's also the emoji I'll send if I am a bit pissed off but I know the other person needs a response. And sometimes I

Chapter Seven: ONLINE AND DIGITAL RELATIONSHIPS

use it if I am having a bad day but don't feel like telling the truth. Because I use it in this way, sometimes, when I receive a 'thumbs up' from someone important to me, like one of my parents or a close friend, I can find myself wondering if I've annoyed them in some way. If you were with someone IRL (in real life) and they answered you with a 'thumbs up', what would you think? It's kind of an ambivalent response – would you need clarification?

USUAL PRACTICE

There isn't a 'usual practice' around online and digital relationships – and by 'usual practice', I mean that there isn't a socially agreed way to approach something that can be fun and pleasurable but also has harmful consequences if misused. For example, socially, we've agreed usual practices around food – in many cultures we eat three meals a day, and, on the whole, sweet foods come after savoury. In the UK we've agreed that smoking cigarettes can be an option for those over 16 as long as people are made aware of the health consequences. Sex is legal from age 16, and alcohol can be consumed by those over the age of 18. You and I both know that lots of us do not stick to these rules, but regardless, they are in place for our safety and for the good of our health and to promote a usual practice.

We now know that the online world is another thing that can be fun and pleasurable but can also have negative health-related consequences. Mental health professionals, including myself, have often talked about how, for the good of future generations' mental and emotional health, online engagement – and specifically social media – needs to be the next thing that usual practice guidelines are created for. Joey Odom, founder of a tech company called Aro even compares the effect screen time has on our health to that of second-hand smoke.

What I find interesting is that most people seem to agree that we are a bit out of our depth when it comes to our online relationships and, as a society we struggle to put the boundaries or a usual practice in place. It took until August 2024 for a major mobile network provider, owned by British Telecom, to be quoted as saying that under 11s should not have access to smartphones. For a phone provider to say that children should not have smartphones seems pretty huge. However, I spoke to Clare Fernyhough, Psychologist and Co-founder of a campaign known as Smartphone Free Childhood. She pointed out that tech companies cannot legally harvest data from under-13s. So, maybe what we really need are informed guidelines and usual practice suggestions from phone providers for people aged 13–16, as well as for adults. The recommendation made likely comes from a building awareness of the negative impact and effects of smartphone and internet usage on children's mental health. I'd still question how much tech businesses are actually doing to help us look after our digital and relational health. From what I know, in short, the answer is still not a lot – in fact many apps available on smartphones are becoming more and more dangerous to young people's wellbeing as it becomes easier to hide interactions from the adults who are supposed to protect them.

There is astoundingly clear evidence that the increase in mental health issues in teens and preteens over the past 20 years is aligned with the how we relate to others online, specifically through social media and starting with the creation of Facebook. The impact is largely due to a lack of awareness around what a usual and healthy practice should look like and how to limit the negative impact that online and digital relationships can have on ourselves and others. I say this a lot, and I stand by it: **the only way to combat this is to be educating young people about mental health as part of the curriculum**. We teach our kids physical education from a very young age, and the same time and effort should go into mental health. If we were all taught how to protect our self-worth, use boundaries, understand when comparisons and distractions are useful and when they are not, and process our feelings, there would be fewer negative outcomes from internet use over time – although it would take a generation to infiltrate society.

One of the other risks of online communication without more knowledge around healthy usual practice, particularly in upcoming generations as they know no different, is that the lack of niceties and increased apathetic reactions can start to seep into our relationships in person. A great deal of the ways we respond online are not socially appropriate in real life. Imagine if you said something to someone which warranted a response, and then two days

Chapter Seven: ONLINE AND DIGITAL RELATIONSHIPS

later they randomly responded without even considering what the silence was like for you. Or what if, in real life, you shared something vulnerable, and the person said nothing and instead made a heart shape with their hands. How would you feel? I know I would feel incredibly exposed and unsafe.

And look at the ways we communicate with artificial intelligence. We basically order AI around and teach tech like Siri and Alexa to stroke our egos. When I first met Siri, I asked them to call me 'Gorgeous Girl' instead of Zoë, and still now when I say: 'Hey Siri, what's my name?', Siri responds with 'It's Zoë but since we're friends, I get to call you Gorgeous Girl.' And I always respond with a smile and feel very proud of myself, but I say nothing back. Gosh, imagine if someone paid me a compliment like that to my face and I just walked away and ended the conversation – I'd have no friends left. Likewise, imagine if you said to your friend Alexa, 'Alexa – order dog food' or 'Alexa – STOP!' as I often find myself shouting through the house when my mind goes into sensory overload and I need some silence. Unless your friend Alexa is a mind reader or a butler, I think they'd be quite offended.

You might be thinking, *but Siri and Alexa are robots, they don't have feelings*. You'd be right. And it's not necessarily a risk for those of us who've already learned the art of socialisation, because we know the difference. However, my generation is the last generation that will know what life is like without online relationships, social media and AI. There are young people being born who are listening to the adults in their lives ordering robots around, calling their satnav 'stupid' and getting angry very quickly and swearing when AI irritates them. Children and babies hear the adults around them talking (it doesn't matter to whom or what) and take that modelled behaviour on as the usual way to do things. So, in terms of usual practice, either we need to be teaching the distinct difference between talking to a robot and talking to a human very early on, or we can teach respect as a rule of thumb regardless of whether the conversation is with AI or a person in real life.

I believe that as part of looking after the mental and relational health of generations to come and making sure they have the ability to make healthy choices about online relationships we need to stay on top of the wider effects and impacts of our online communication. Because tech has infiltrated our world to such an extent that we are almost always connected to our online worlds, working towards a usual practice that allows us to live digitally healthy lifestyles is essential. One really effective boundary you can hold that will get you started is to speak as similarly as you would during a face-to-face conversation when you are communicating online or with AI. This limits the potential for increased social awkwardness as well as anxiety filtering through into in-person relationships from online relationships. It also teaches the same usual practice to any little ears that might be listening.

There are other reasons we need usual practice guidelines in this arena that I haven't delved into here because they are beyond the scope of this chapter. These include but are not limited to: being targeted by bullies and trolls; identity theft; phishing; scams; downloading cyber viruses; getting involved in the dark web; and posting things that you regret in later life. But I will now discuss one particular key risk: the risk of developing a screen or internet addiction.

RECOGNISING SCREEN AND INTERNET ADDICTION

Internet or screen addiction is a term we to use to describe a pathological dependency on TV, apps and video games – as well as anything internet related, including porn, shopping, gambling, social media and communication. Much of the theory surrounding addiction which I've covered in previous chapters applies here too. If you are experiencing cravings (a compulsive need to check or look at things online), an increase in tolerance (the amount of time you stay attached to your screen and/or the internet), and withdrawal symptoms (which may show up as anxiety, a feeling of dread, panic attacks and depression), plus detrimental effects on your wellbeing due to your screen or internet use, your relationship to your digital and online behaviour may be in the realms of an addiction.

One reason that screens and the internet are so addictive is that without them, quite simply, we'd have to be more tolerant, have a lot more patience, and do a lot more waiting. How many times this week have you shut down a webpage or an app because it's taking more than a few seconds to load? Not having to wait for longer than a nanosecond for a need or want to be met is a development that has only happened in the past two decades – 20 years ago we had to wait... sometimes for whole minutes, for the internet to connect and pages to load. If that was still the case, how on earth would I distract myself? I wouldn't be able to open Instagram for a couple of minutes when my mind gets tired of writing, watch a few reels about cats and read some empowering quotes, before returning to what I was doing. I'd have to stay focused, or maybe just stare into space. But my mind is used to the stimulation now, so my default, when I start running out of steam or feel a need to be distracted, is to go straight to my smartphone. If it takes longer than a nanosecond to load, I notice that I tend to lose interest. I also notice that it is hard for me to wait. When I decide I need/want to buy something, I feel the need to do it right there and then. Twenty years ago, I'd have made a shopping list, waited until the weekend and gone shopping with a group of friends to get the things I wanted – it was a far more social event.

The quicker our online connections have become, the less patience we have in general. The less patience we have in general, the less tolerance we have for ourselves and other people online and in real life. The less tolerance we have for others, the more likely it is that we will choose to sort things out in isolation rather than making it a social opportunity: it directly impacts our social skills. The instantaneous nature of being online these days means that we are now conditioned for instant gratification. We are not used to tolerating the space between asking for a need to be met and that need being met.

Children and screen addiction
Most adults I know (but not all) display some level of internet and screen addiction but because it's (relatively speaking) a new behaviour formed following a couple of decades of in person socialisation, a lot of us can find ways to manage it without too many negative consequences on our health. The worrying trend nowadays is that as generation Z move into their young

adulthood, we are starting to see the long-term consequences of internet and screen addiction on the psychological and social development of children and young people who haven't lived without technology.

Biologically speaking, time spent online can contribute to a reduction in the all-important bonding hormone, oxytocin. When we connect with someone in person, we experience a release of oxytocin and we feel fondness, love, joy, understanding and all those nice things. Digital and online relationships don't offer this opportunity as they are often carried out in isolation. The lack of authentic human connection can result in diminished oxytocin supply, the effect being, quite simply that we feel less and less likeable and loveable but continue to seek to get our connection needs met by spending more and more time online, thus we are becoming more and more unhappy.

Because we're all seeking connections via social media, it's considered normal and there are a wealth of other things to blame for the state of our mental health, so it's easy to dismiss and close the cognitive dissonance (see p.122) we experience around it. Gen Z however have lived childhoods where they had access to technology without boundaries and they are suffering the consequences in both their online and in-person relationships mainly due to low self-esteem and a need for constant external validation. If you have young children who are part of Generation Alpha, you may be able to see the dangers emerging more clearly. There are more and more reports of primary school-aged children showing symptoms of mental health issues like eating disorders, self-harm, anxiety, depression and screen addiction. However, I would argue that it's the latter that is causing much of the former due to the impact that being online can have on our dopamine and oxytocin levels.

Here's the hard and fast truth – it's not the kids, they haven't done this to themselves, it's us as parents, educators, caregivers and tech companies enabling an addictive substance that we, as adults, don't even really understand how to navigate yet. We need to get our heads around the fact that when we give children access to screens, regardless of how you justify it, we set them up to become addicted.

Chapter Seven: ONLINE AND DIGITAL RELATIONSHIPS

What became very clear when I spoke with Clare Fernyhough about her campaign was just how abusive and addictive the relationship between children and the digital world can be. Social media platforms in particular are, quite frankly, creating more and more opportunities for addiction and a chronic need for external validation to flourish. In particular, Clare compared putting smartphones into the hands of children with allowing them to experiment with drugs and alcohol, which, to my earlier point, the majority of people would not do because it is not usual practice for a child to experiment with drugs and alcohol so young and the consequences could be dire.

Admittedly, it's a hard one to navigate because no one wants their children to be missing out, but we do need to be teaching kids how to handle the technology available to them without becoming addicted. Much of the pressure to expose children to an addictive and predatory online world comes from the tech companies themselves. Children do not need tech to improve their quality of life and emotional wellbeing – they need strong and loving primary relationships that support their biological need for connection and validation, so they don't have to seek it in other, more dangerous places.

As terrifying as it is, you'll know if a child is on the way towards screen addiction if, when you take the screen away, a stress response (fight, flight, freeze) is triggered, and/or they react with a level of anger that shocks you. Adults feel the same when something we are hooked on gets taken away – we just hide it better and often have the skills to manipulate the situation to satisfy our cravings.

How can you tell whether you're addicted to the screen itself or what's on the screen?
In its most basic form, you can self-diagnose your screen and internet addiction by considering if your relationship with the screen or what's on the screen is interfering with your physical, relational and mental health. For some, it's about the porn, the game or the emails. For others, it doesn't matter what's on the screen; it's the screen itself and the dissociation from reality that is addictive.

You can self-assess how addictive your relationship is with either by considering the following:

Examples of being addicted to what's on the screen:
- If you are spending more time playing online video games than spending time with your family
- If the porn you are watching is negatively impacting the intimacy in your romantic relationship
- If your online shopping habit means you are spending more money than you have
- If you are checking your work emails because you convince yourself it will make tomorrow easier – whereas in fact it just makes now worse because you're not present with your in-person relationships
- If you find yourself compulsively scrolling through social media, comparing your life to what you see online, and it's having a negative impact on your self-esteem

Examples of being addicted to the screen itself:
- If you find yourself not looking after yourself physically (not showering, eating or exercising) because you can't get away from your screen
- You 'lose time' when you are online
- You double or triple screen – watching TV and playing on your phone without really focusing on either

Whether it's the screen or what's on the screen, additional physical issues can arise, like your eyes hurting, headaches, insomnia, dehydration and poor posture. This, or any of the above, means that your mental and physical health is suffering due to your use of screens. You might also start missing out on things like daylight, or you may forget to attend an appointment or event due to your compulsion to be online.

In terms of recovering from screen addiction, it can be helpful to know which category is more problematic for you. Only you really know which is true. Either way, the underlying issue is usually the same. Your experience is that your screen, or what's on it, helps you manage your feelings and takes you away from your intimate interpersonal relationships.

Chapter Seven: ONLINE AND DIGITAL RELATIONSHIPS

Exercise: Setting bottom lines in recovery from screen and internet addiction

If you think you might have an internet or screen addiction, try setting some 'bottom lines' (a common term used in addiction recovery circles). See if you can stick to them. If it feels too difficult, then you may need professional help to support you in understanding why. Choose three online-related behaviours that are causing you pain.

For example:

- *Compulsively online gaming*
- *Spending money online*
- *Scrolling through social media when you should be sleeping*

Decide what the behaviour you want to bottom line is. For example:

- *No online gaming*
- *No impulse buying online – it has to be a planned, thought-out decision*
- *No social media after you've brushed your teeth, or indeed a certain time of your choosing*

Make sure your bottom lines are realistic and see if you can stick to them for a month. After a month, explore any changes you've noticed in yourself and decide if you want to continue with your bottom line in any form, be that keeping them as they are or adjusting them to fit as time goes on.

This is harder than it sounds written down here. Please expect there to be times when it feels really difficult – those are the moments that matter and the ones that make lasting change.

DIGITAL HEALTH

I'll start to end this chapter with an adapted definition of digital health that I helped put together whilst I was working with the computer software company I mentioned earlier: *Digital health in-*

volves building a balanced, effective and beneficial state of wellbeing within our relationship with technology.

Thinking about your digital health choices in line with your relational health means assessing your habits and consumption, and looking at what can help you feel more fulfilled in your digital and online relationships.

There's been a shift in the past five years towards the need to balance both online activities and how available we are to other people online. Rather than being eternally accessible online or switched off entirely, and therefore struggling with digital boundaries, we need balance to be conceivable. When you're digitally healthy, you get to choose what your relationship with being online and your online relationships looks like day to day, based on what you know about yourself at that time.

Research conducted as part of the digital health campaign I was involved with, in late 2020, involving over 2,000 adults in the UK (piloted by Opinion Matters on behalf of Microsoft, using 2000+ UK adults, between 30th October – 3rd November 2020, see Further Reading) showed that people who do find a balanced, effective and beneficial state of wellbeing within their digital lives have been able to use technology to discover a new interest, skill, passion or hobby. They are also seen to be connecting with like-minded people, in other words, maintaining healthy online relationships. All good stuff!

As a result of these findings, I think about digital health on a sliding scale that is always evolving, rather than something we can just switch on or off from. Thinking about it as evolving and ongoing helps to prevent a feeling of being overwhelmed, and protects our overall mental, relational and digital health.

On top of all I have shared with you so far in this chapter, one of my most simple and favourite therapeutic tools for helping people balance their online relationships is to use a traffic light system. I came up with it on the spot when troubleshooting with how to support employees with their mental health for a British digital rail and coach technology platform.

I suggest it here because being online can be particularly draining, but you can use a traffic light system to help manage your energy levels online. It goes a bit like this:

Chapter Seven: ONLINE AND DIGITAL RELATIONSHIPS

You can be at Green, Amber or Red

- Green means you are feeling energised, focused and you have a lot to give.
- Amber means you are having a slower online day.
- Red means you're not in a good enough place to be communicating online today.

Where you are on that list at any time depends on various things: how much sleep you've had, your emotional state, physical activity, levels of anxiety, and the environmental cues you have around you.

If you are having a Red day, you can hold a boundary around avoiding social media or dating apps. Admittedly, with online workplace relationships, it's less easy to hold a boundary that says, 'I won't be using that app today' and getting back to people tomorrow, and so, if you have to, I suggest attending your online calls and meetings as expected and, where you can, take a back seat elsewhere to counterbalance where you're at. For example, if you were due to lead a meeting, be present and ask if someone else can lead or, lead the meeting if you must but ensure you know how you are going to compensate yourself for it – maybe take a morning offline later in the week. You can also be honest about your capacity that day and tell people you'll be taking notes and will respond in full on a different day. A word of advice, apply this with confidence and from your functional adult ego-state (see pp. 140-141). People tend not to respond well to these types of boundaries if you set them from a victim-like position and you may end up on the Drama Triangle (see pp. 143-7).

I encourage you to come up with your own examples here, as inevitably I won't fully understand what your personal digital health or online relationships look like and indeed I do not have all the details and nuances of what else is going on that may also impact your choices.

In conclusion, there is clearly still a significant gap in our knowledge about how to make healthy lifestyle choices online and understand why we choose the people (or algorithims) we choose along the way.

On reflection I feel this final chapter feels as if it moved us away from our primary question: *why do we choose the people we choose?* To my mind that is because there is so much more learning and preventative work that needs to be understood in this particular niche. Having said that we can still take the time to apply everything we know about ourselves, and about the other types of in-person realtionships we've explored to support our understanding in why we make the choices we make online, be that about choosing people or our own behaviours, and how to change them if we want to. I look forward to a future where people feel less controlled by algorithms and more in control of what they want online.

Summary

1. *Most of our relationships these days are a hybrid of online and in person.*
2. *You can use online connections to help you work through anxiety as well as create it.*
3. *Having a set of boundaries around online relationships can help support your mental, relational and digital health.*
4. *Be mindful about your online behaviour and investigate if it would translate well into in-person behaviour.*
5. *Healthy digital and online relationships are about finding balance and fulfilment, just like other relationships. Do the work to make sure you know how to get your needs met and feel fulfilled and nourished.*

A FINAL NOTE

Not everything in this book will work for everyone, and I know there are many things I haven't been able to cover or expand on in great detail. I recognise that as a white, female, heterosexual, cis-gendered, able-bodied person, there is a lot I don't cover. But I do hope what you've read here has been as inclusive as possible and provided insight as to how to create more choice in your life.

In reality, I feel like each chapter in this book could have been a book in its own right. I've included as much information as I can within the constraints of one chapter per type of relationship. There is of course far more information accessible to you through further reading, therapy and online. I am always happy to help, so if you feel you need support navigating anything you've read, please reach out to me via my website www.zoeaston.com or on social media www.instagram.com/zoeastondotcom.

I hope you've learned about your feelings and behaviours in relationships, and how they are shaped by your past and your present. Whether you've skim-read most of this or got stuck into the work, on one level or another, you've likely become aware of considerable adjustments you might like to make work over the past 216 pages. Please don't be tempted to try and change everything at once. Take just one thing at a time and work on that. The rest will follow.

The big take aways from all seven chapters is first that your self-worth is inherent, it does not need to be earned. The second is that our relationship with **our self is defined by the state of our self-worth, and the state of our self-worth defines how we show up in relation to others.** In relationships with others, our defences can be both created and evoked. Trauma, fears and vulnerabilities can be activated within us, as well as healed. Damage done in relationships heals through relationships.

That said, please do not worry if things feel like they are changing too slowly. I often have clients who've found themselves in a familiar and unhealthy relationship dynamic after a block of therapy to support them to extrapolate themselves from exactly that. They say to me, 'I thought I'd worked through this!'. So, let me reassure you – **you are working through it** – and you may always be doing so. Sometimes we are presented with one or more final 'tests' to see if you really do want to change and sometimes it's the perfect opportunity to make different/new choices and rewrite your script, other times they happen so you can continue to learn. Difficulties don't vanish because you talked about them or read about them – you just understand what has happened to you more deeply, and therefore have more choices about how you behave. And... **choice is the opposite of trauma.**

If there was just one thing I would ask you to stay aware of, it would be this: Change is inevitable. We all change over time, and part of the intimacy of relationships involves understanding and working with change.

Most of us find change hard because whenever there is change there is loss and – even if the change is objectively positive – whenever there is loss, there is grief. Part of learning to cope with relationships changing over time means allowing yourself to grieve the parts that are gone, and welcome in the new.

It's always helped me to hold in mind that change is a type of ending. You will go through a subtle or not-so-subtle grieving process. I've done my best to encapsulate what this might look for you below:

Five stages of grief
Based on the Kübler-Ross model.

Denial *may show up when a relationship is changing or breaking down, as well as if someone has passed away. It can look like you ignoring the changes, and assuming you and/or the other person/people are able to maintain the relationship as it was before things changed. Denial is vital however because it's a psychological mechanism that allows you to process information at a pace that you can cope with.*

Anger *comes in many forms. Everything from being a bit pissed off to total rage comes under the anger umbrella. This includes feeling annoyed, irritated, frustrated, provoked, exasperated... the list goes on. We have to feel our anger when grieving – be it towards the person, or the situation – in order to move through it.*

A FINAL NOTE

Bargaining *is when you start trying to fill in the gaps to make sense of what has happened and change the outcome. For example: saying things like 'If only I hadn't sent that message', 'I take back what I said, I didn't mean it', or 'Let's just go for a drink and forget about it'. It's a way of attempting to feel in control of the situation again. If a person has passed away, you might be more likely to find yourself thinking along the lines of 'what ifs' and 'if onlys' as you try to make sense of what's happened by filling in the gaps in the narrative.*

Depression *can be activated when you realise you are not in control of a situation, and experience low feelings. To be clear, depression is usually diagnosed if you've been experiencing a low mood for about 50 per cent of the time over a period of several weeks and it's impacting your day-to-day life. It is thought to be born out of the repression of emotion. Not everyone will plummet into full-blown clinical depression when a relationship changes or ends, but most of us will feel upset and sad about it if we allow ourselves to and, maybe ironically, it's the allowing ourselves to feel the feelings that can prevent a full-blown depression. Plus, allowing yourself to be in touch with your emotions increases the intimacy in your relationship with yourself, and can give you huge opportunities to grow, as hard as it can be.*

Acceptance *is an active process that you have to consciously decide to do each day until it becomes automatic. Don't be fooled into thinking you'll get to a place of acceptance by waiting for it to happen. If you are proactive in your choices and you've allowed yourself to process the other stages of grief along the way, you get to choose acceptance when it becomes available. Additionally, acceptance isn't always a positive emotional experience. In some experiences feelings of anger and sadness can hang around even when you're in a place of acceptance. Put differently, acceptance doesn't take away your feelings, but it helps you move forward with them.*

It was originally thought that these five stages always happen in this order. We now know that they do not. Change and therefore grief is a messy process, and you will move back and forward between different stages, revisiting the one you are most familiar with more often. And I use the word 'familiar' in its truest form – the stage of grief most present in your family of origin (FOO) will likely be the one that feels like it'll get you what you want.

The best way to identify your most familiar stage of grief is to think about what you did in your FOO to change things that you didn't like. For example, if you became angry when a caregiver said 'no' to you, and they gave in, you'll likely spend most of your time in the anger stage when trying to process grief, potentially expecting things to change. Likewise, if bargaining tended to get your desired result, that is where you'll revert. The issue with being stuck in a familiar stage of grief is that, well, you stay stuck there. This is most likely because in childhood, whenever your caregiver gave into your behaviour, you didn't get the chance to practise moving through all the stages. You can really help yourself move on from the grief that happens with changing relationships by giving yourself permission to work through each stage.

To close: I often tell people that therapy is a bit like planting a wild garden. As the therapist, I throw a lot of mud and seeds at you in the form of information. You won't retain it all – in fact I think we only retain around an average of 20 per cent of the information we are given straight away; the rest, however, is planted. Days, weeks, months, and even years from now, some of those seeds might flower and you'll get a lightbulb moment that you didn't see coming. So, give yourself grace as well as time. All the seeds I've introduced to you here are slowly growing their roots and will eventually flower, whether you are aware of it or not.

FURTHER READING AND WEBLINKS

INTRODUCTION

Further Reading
- Brené Brown, *Atlas of the Heart* (Ebury Digital, 2021)
- Anna Mueller and Seth Abrutyn, *Life Under Pressure: The Social Roots of Youth Suicide and What to Do About Them* (OUP, 2024)
- Rory O'Connor, *When it is Darkest: Why People Die by Suicide and What We Can Do to Prevent It* (Ebury Digital, 2021)
- Abraham H Maslow, *A Theory of Human Motivation* (Grapevine India, 2022)

Weblinks
- Definition of Relationships – tinyurl.com/4d94zaxp
- Definition of Bonds – tinyurl.com/3ehttpvb
- The Gendlin Online Library: The works of Eugene T. Gendlin – focusing.org/gendlin/gol_intro.html

Chapter One: SELF

Further Reading
- Zoë Aston, *Your Mental Health Workout* (Yellow Kite, 2021)
- Sarah Ockwell-Smith, *Because I said so* (Piatkus, 2023)
- Rupert Brown, *Henri Tajfel: Explorer of Identity and Difference* (Routledge, 2019)
- Carl Rogers, *On Becoming a Person* (Robinson, 1961)
- Roy Baumeister, *The Self in Social Psychology* (Routledge, 2000)
- Mark Muraven & Roy Baumeister, *Self-regulation and Depletion of Limited Resources: Does Self-control Resemble a Muscle?* (American Psychological Association, 2000)
- Pia Mellody, *Facing Codependence: What It Is, Where It Comes From, How It Sabotages Our Lives* (PublisDrive, 2002)

Weblinks
- Chartand and Barth, 'The chameleon effect: The perception–behavior link and social interaction' (1999) – psycnet.apa.org/record/1999-05479-002
- Julianne Holt-Lunstad, Timothy B Smith, J Bradley Layton, 'Social relationships and mortality risk: a meta-analytic review' (2010) – pubmed.ncbi.nlm.nih.gov/20668659/

Chapter Two: BOUNDARIES, WANTS AND NEEDS AND ATTACHMENT TYPES

Further Reading
- Amir Levine and Rachel S F Heller, *Attached: Are you anxious, avoidant or secure? How the science of adult attachment can help you find and keep love* (Bluebird, 2011)
- Daniel J Siegel and Tina Payne Bryson, *The Power of Showing Up* (Scribe, 2020)
- John Bowlby, *A Secure Base* (Routledge, 2005)

Weblinks
- Harlow's Classic Studies Revealed the Importance of Maternal Contacy (2018) – www.psychologicalscience.org/publications/observer/obsonline/harlows-classic-studies-revealed-the-importance-of-maternal-contact.html

Chapter Three: FAMILY RELATIONSHIPS

Further Reading
- Pia Mellody, *Facing Codependence: What It Is, Where It Comes from, How It Sabotages Our Lives* (PublishDrive, 2002)
- Melody Beattie, *The New Codependency: Help and Guidance for Today's Generation* (Simon and Schuster, 2009)
- Sarah Ockwell-Smith, *The Gentle Parenting Book: How to raise calmer, happier children from birth to seven* (Piatkus, 2016)
- Tian Dayton, *The ACOA Trauma Syndrome: The Impact of Childhood Pain on Adult Relationships* (Health Communications Inc EB, 2012)
- Nessa Carey, *The Epigenetics Revolution* (Icon Books, 2011)
- Sue Gerhardt, *Why Love Matters* (Routledge, 2014)
- Gabor Maté, Daniel Maté, *The Myth of Normal: Illness, Health and Healing in a Toxic Culture* (Ebury Digital, 2022)
- Philippa Perry, *The Book You Wish Your Parents Had Read* (Penguin, 2019)

Weblinks
- K.L. Workman - When Helping Hurts: Validating a Measure of Compulsive Helping and Exploring Potential Predictors (2022) – scholarsarchive.byu.edu/cgi/viewcontent.cgi?article=11131&context=etd

Chapter Four: FRIENDSHIPS

Further Reading
- Lisa Feldman Barrett, *How Emotions Are Made: The Secret Life of the Brain* (Picador, 2017)

FURTHER READING AND WEBLINKS

- Tanith Carey, *The Friendship Maze* (Vie, 2019)
- Zoë Aston, *Your Mental Health Workout* (Yellow Kite, 2021)
- Elizabeth Day, *Friendaholic: Confessions of a Friendship Addict* (Fourth Estate, 2023)
- Elaine Aron, *The Highly Sensitive Person: How to Survive and Thrive When the World Overwhelms You* (Thorsons, 2014)
- Robin Dunbar, *Friends: Understanding the Power of Our Most Important Relationships* (Little, Brown Book Group, 2021)

Weblinks

- Karmel W. Choi, Ph.D., An Exposure-Wide and Mendelian Randomization Approach to Identifying Modifiable Factors for the Prevention of Depression (2020) – ajp.psychiatryonline.org/doi/10.1176/appi.ajp.2020.19111158
- Jo Williams, The compass of shame (2019) – practice-supervisors.rip.org.uk/wp-content/uploads/2019/11/The-compass-os-shame.pdf

Chapter Five: ROMANTIC RELATIONSHIPS

Further Reading

- Moira Weigel, *Labour of Love: The Invention of Dating* (Farrar, Straus and Giroux, 2016)
- Nell Frizzell, *The Panic Years* (Transworld Digital, 2021)
- Gary Chapman, *The 5 Love Languages: The Secret to Love That Lasts* (Moody Publishers, 2010)
- Pia Mellody, Andrea Wells Miller, J Keith Miller, *Facing Love Addiction* (HarperOne, 2003)
- Pia Mellody, Lawrence S Freundlich, *The Intimacy Factor* (HarperOne, 2009)
- Karen Gurney, *Mind The Gap: The Truth About Desire and How to Futureproof Your Sex Life* (Headline Home, 2020)
- McCurry, May & Donaldson, Both partners negative emotion drives aggression during couples conflict, (Communications Psychology, 2024)

Weblinks

- Sex and Love Addicts Anonymous – slaauk.org/
- Larry Getlen, The Fascinating history of how courtship became 'dating' (2016) – nypost.com/2016/05/15/the-fascinating-history-of-how-courtship-became-dating/
- Dr. Marni Feuerman, Managing vs. Resolving Conflict in Relationships: The Blueprints for Success (2017) – www.gottman.com/blog/managing-vs-resolving-conflict-relationships/

Chapter Six: **WORKPLACE RELATIONSHIPS**

Further Reading
- Brené Brown, *Atlas of the Heart* (Ebury Digital, 2021)
- Leon Festinger, *A Theory of Cognitive Dissonance* (Stanford University Press, 1957)
- L S Leach, C Poyser, P Butterworth, 'Workplace bullying and the association with suicidal ideation/thoughts and behaviour: a systematic review', in *Occupational and Environmental Medicine* (2017)
- Gerstick, Bartunek and Dutton, *Learning from Academia: The Importance of Relationships in Professional Life* (Academy of Management Journal, 2004)
- Schandura and Meuser, *Relational Dynamics of Leadership: Problems and Prospects* (Annual Reviews, 2021)
- Kim and Plester, *Ironing Out the Differences: The Role of Humour in Workplace Relationships* (Springer, 2015)
- Gary Chapman and Paul White, *The 5 Languages of Appreciation in the Workplace* (Moody Publishers, 2012)
- Richard Robb, *Willful: How We Choose What We Do* (Yale University Press, 2019)
- Michael Easter, *Scarcity Brain* (Headline Home, 2023)
- Raja and Stein, *Work-Life Balance: History, Costs and Budgeting for Balance* (Thieme Medical Publishers, 2014)
- John Bradshaw, *Healing the Shame That Binds You* (Health Communications Inc., 2005)

Weblinks
- Joshua Luna, The toxic effects of branding your workplace a 'family' (2021) – hbr.org/2021/10/the-toxic-effects-of-branding-your-workplace-a-family
- Griffiths, Demetrovics and Atroszko, Ten Myths about Work Addiction (2018) – akjournals.com/view/journals/2006/7/4/article-p845.xml
- Stanley Milgram, Obedience Experiment (1963) – www.simplypsychology.org/milgram.html

Documentary
- *Simone Biles Rising*, Netflix (2024)

Chapter Seven: **ONLINE AND DIGITAL RELATIONSHIPS**

Further Reading
- Anthony Elliott, *Algorithmic Intimacy: The Digital Revolution in Personal Relationships* (Polilty, 2022)
- Zoë Aston, *Your Mental Health Workout* (Yellow Kite, 2021)

FURTHER READING AND WEBLINKS

Weblinks

- Yuquian Zhou, 'The Benefits and Dangers of Online Dating Apps' (2023) – www.researchgate.net/publication/366786260_The_Benefits_and_Dangers_of_Online_Dating_Apps #:~:text=It%20explores%20the%20advantages%20and,finding%20a%20match%20is%20guaranteed
- Corey Johnson, 'Sexual violence and abuse in online dating: A scoping review' (2022) – www.academia.edu/84818209/Sexual_violence_and_abuse_in_online_dating_A_scoping_review?hb-g-sw=105545528
- Microsoft Research (2020) – www.microsoft.com/en-us/research/theme/digital-mental-health/publications/
- Younes et al, 'Internet Addiction and Relationships with Insomnia, Anxiety, Depression, Stress and Self-Esteem in University Students: A Cross-Sectional Designed Study' (2016) – journals.plos.org/plosone/article?id=10.1371/journal.pone.0161126
- Sara Thomee, 'Mobile Phone Use and Mental Health. A Review of the Research That Takes a Psychological Perspective on Exposure' (2018) – www.mdpi.com/1660-4601/15/12/2692
- K Demirci, et al, 'Relationship of smartphone use severity with sleep quality, depression, and anxiety in university students' (2015) – akjournals.com/view/journals/2006/4/2/article-p85.xml
- Choski and Patel, 'A Study to Find Out the Correlation of Mobile Phone Addiction with Anxiety, Depression, Stress and Sleep Quality in the College Students of Surat City' (2019) – tiny.cc/7p09zz
- Lucy Hooker, 'EE tells parents: don't give under-11s smartphones' (2024) – www.bbc.co.uk/news/articles/c4gvpy3yz1yo
- Smartphone Free Childhood – smartphonefreechildhood.co.uk

WHERE TO FIND FURTHER SUPPORT

Find a therapist
- BACP therapist directory – www.bacp.co.uk/search/Therapists
- Psychology Today therapist directory – www.psychologytoday.com

Dysfunctional Families Support
- Find a support group – www.psychologytoday.com/gb/groups
- ACA (an inclusive organisation open to all affected by family dysfunction) – www.adultchildrenofalcoholics.co.uk
- Meet up topic for dysfunction families – www.meetup.com/topics/dysfunctfamilies/

Eating Disorder Support
- www.beateatingdisorders.org.uk/
- www.oagb.org.uk/
- aba12steps.org/

Suicide awareness and support
- www.nhs.uk/mental-health/feelings-symptoms-behaviours/behaviours/help-for-suicidal-thoughts/
- www.nimh.nih.gov/health/topics/suicide-prevention

Breaking Free from Trauma and Trauma Bonds support
- www.thehotline.org/resources/trauma-bonds-what-are-they-and-how-can-we-overcome-them/
- www.gov.uk/guidance/domestic-abuse-how-to-get-help

Internet and Screen Addiction Support
- www.internetaddictsanonymous.org
- www.nightingalehospital.co.uk/technology-addiction

Work Addiction Support
- www.wa-uk.org

Sex and Love Addiction Support
- www.slaauk.org

WHERE TO FIND FURTHER SUPPORT

If you're struggling right now

- Mind 0300 102 1234 – open 9am – 6pm weekdays
- Samaritans 116 123 – always open
- Campaign Against Living Miserably 0800 58 58 58 – Open 5pm – midnight
- If you're in Wales: CALL 0800 132 737 – always open
- If you're under 25: text THEMIX to 85258 – always open

GLOSSARY

Childism: An ism you may not be familiar with… yet. It refers to the power exchange and disrespect between adults and children. It's a largely dismissed topic, but not entirely new. Acknowledging childism means acknowledging that we have all been treated badly by people older than us at some point in our lives. (See Further Reading: *Because I Said So.*)

Classical Conditioning: A process in which stimuli are psychologically connected to each other through a learned experience. Experiments including Pavlov's dogs and Little Albert are famous for proving this theory.

Co-dependency: When a person is compulsively dependent on other people to make them feel okay. Often, they are in a relationship with a partner who is unwell either emotionally or physically. As with most things, co-dependency runs on a spectrum: there's the too-dependent co-dependent and the anti-dependent co-dependent. Both usually display an intense need to look after and be looked after by other people and experience high levels of anger and anxiety when their help is not gratefully received. Co-dependency always stems from our Family of Origin (FOO).

Co-regulation: When someone else supports us to regulate our physical and psychological needs. We are born helpless and vulnerable and would not survive as a species without co-regulation. As we age, we are able to self-regulate and become less dependent on others to help get our needs met.

Counter-transference: When a therapist has feelings about the client they are working with. When used well, these feelings can help the therapist to understand the client's relationships better. Without that awareness, however, counter-transference can mean that the therapist has trouble remaining objective and can get caught up in the client's dysfunction.

Defences: In therapy we explore what are known as defence mechanisms. These unconscious reactions help you tolerate or defend against difficult emotions like fear, shame, loneliness, anger and sadness. Defences also help you to ignore things that you don't want to think about or cope with, like a painful history or specific event. Pretty much any behaviour can be a defence; from laughing to rage attacks, it all depends on the context. Lots of mental health issues such as addictions, eating disorders and even psychosis can develop out of a need to defend ourselves from our reality. Cutting out friends, ghosting people and dissociation (see below) are also types of psychological defences.

Dissociation: A psychological process of disconnecting from your feelings, thoughts, memories and self. We all dissociate at times, but chronic episodes of dissociation may indicate further issues including identity disorders.

Ego states: A way of understanding what is going on inside of us, based on what we know about our history and the context we are currently in. They are defined by a consistent pattern of thinking, feeling and behaving.

GLOSSARY

Empathy: The ability to understand another person's thoughts and feelings, as well as your own. It differs from sympathy, where you effectively join the other person and feel their feelings for them. People often reject sympathy because it's not helpful. Empathy, however, is usually well received.

Enmeshment: A relational experience where two (or more) people have a sense that they are the same as each other. When enmeshed, you might struggle to have boundaries, believe someone else can read your mind, and lose a sense of autonomy that affects your development.

Envious Attacks: Are rooted in low self-esteem and occur when the envious person is feeling less than another person. The 'attack' is an attempt to make the other person feel as bad about themselves as the attacker does. They can take the form of an overt or covert put down, saying things like 'I told you so' and disguising cruel sarcastic comments as jokes.

Familiar: Aside from the usual definition of 'familiar' (something that is well known to you), if you break down the word – FAMILI-AR – you literally get the word 'famili(y)'. Most of the things you find familiar in relationships, good and bad, will stem from your 'family(ar)'.

Family of Creation: The family you go on to make – your children and partner, be that a wife, husband, partner or co-parent.

Felt sense: A concept originally developed by Eugene Gendlin as part of his 'focusing' technique, the 'felt sense' functions as a connection between the mind and body. The idea is that you can feel things in your body better than you can think them in your brain. When 'it just feels right or wrong' but you can't explain why – that's your felt sense kicking in.

Gaslighting: The act of trying to convince someone else that they are the ones with an issue. For example, denying something even though there is evidence to prove it. It tends to make the victim question their sanity and doubt themselves, their memory and their perception.

Groupthink: A mode of thinking in small cohesive groups, such as families, where an unhelpful way of thinking about or viewing a situation is considered the consensus for everyone in the group – whether or not it is valid, correct or helpful. Groupthink enables families to sweep things like abuse under the rug.

Healthy narcissism: Directly related to self-esteem and self-worth without the traits of self-interest becoming pathological. Being able to appreciate your face, body, mind and soul are all traits of healthy narcissism and also contribute to strong self-esteem.

Homeostasis: A self-regulating process by which your body and mind aim to maintain internal stability and balance while adjusting to changing external conditions and experiences. The experience of feeling stressed is often a physiological reaction to our internal experience being off balance for too long. It tells us that homeostasis hasn't been reached through usual means.

Interdependence: Alowing yourself to depend on someone else, and them on you without becoming enmeshed. The best way to think about interdependence is that no one person can meet all of your needs, and some of your needs will need to be met by yourself. Therefore, rather than being totally dependent on one other person, or totally dependent on yourself, you move between the two.

Imposter Syndrome: An ongoing difficulty in feeling that you do not deserve your success and achievements. Or that somehow, you've achieved something due to someone else's merit rather than your own.

Internal conflict: This refers to the psychological experiences of feeling split between two parts of yourself. It can create a dissonant space which puts a huge amount of pressure on the mind to regain balance.

Internal family systems: Developed by Richard Schwartz, this therapeutic approach helps identify and address how people internalise the individuals in their family and the defences or adaptations created around them. The focus, which is to restore balance and heal historical wounds by adjusting the internal dynamics experienced by the individual.

Internalisation: The process of integrating, into your sense of self, the views, attitudes, standards, judgements and opinions that come from other people.

Introjections: The unconscious adoption of thoughts or beliefs via other people. It's a normal part of childhood development to take on parental values and attitudes, but it can also be damaging if a parent's attitude towards something is unhelpful, toxic or even abusive.

Lack Mentality or scarcity mindset: Where you live in the belief that your resources and capacity are limited, and that you're unable to meet certain goals so you don't try.

Love bombing: The act of lavishing someone with attention to fuel the conscious or unconscious motivation to influence and/or manipulate them in order to meet your own emotional needs.

Martyrdom: A term used to describe someone who engages in an activity and exaggerates their suffering around it, in order to obtain sympathy.

Modelling: A process of social learning. The use of the word in psychology means we imitate our role models and behave as we see others behaving in social situations.

Narcissism: Often understood as being a very negative trait, usually because it involves a level of self-obsession and self-interest beyond what most people would consider normal. It is, however, a normal trait of young babies and children – as well as a mental disorder; we all have traits of narcissism, especially when we are scared, stressed and dysregulated. There is also such a thing as healthy narcissism (see above entry) which enables someone to maintain levels of self-interest without exploiting others along the way.

Negative Reinforcement: This refers to an action that removes a negative response. For example, putting an umbrella up when it is raining is a negative reinforcer because it removes something undesirable, namely getting soaked in the rain. The desired outcome is

GLOSSARY

achieved by removing a stimuli, rather than adding one in.

Neuroplasticity: A word used to describe how the brain and nervous system can reorganise itself if it needs to, following a traumatic incident or when it recognises the need for adaptation.

Positive reinforcement: The process of rewarding and reinforcing something desirable in order to increase the likelihood of it happening again. Desirable emotions can be positive reinforcers; when we feel good about something, we tend to want to repeat it.

Power dynamics: When individuals exercise control over others and impact others' social position.

Projection: The process of attaching something that is in your own mind to someone or something else.

Re-parenting: A form of psychotherapy used to treat childhood trauma as well as any adverse life experiences within relationships. The therapist intentionally takes on the role of a parental figure for the client, so that they can learn to develop a nurturing and loving internal parent of their own.

Rejection Sensitivity: A label sometimes given to someone who, more often than usual, perceives and expects to be rejected. This perception may be real or have its roots in something real, but it may also be a perception.

Relational aggression: A type of aggressive behaviour acted out in relation to someone else with the effect of damaging relationships or social position. The observable behaviour can be as subtle as a dirty look or as obvious as humiliating and bullying.

Relational dynamic: The thoughts, feelings and emotions you have when relating to others. They are influenced mainly by your personal relationship history, starting from the day you were born.

Relational Post-Traumatic Stress Disorder (PTSD): A pathological reaction to a stressful or traumatic event that occured within a relationship. It means that your amygdala is activated and you respond with a flight, fight, freeze or fawn response when you meet certain triggers in other people.

Repetition compulsion: An unconscious drive to repeat painful historical events in an attempt to re-enact and repair what happened. Sometimes also called trauma re-enactment.

Self-regulation: When you are able to observe your emotions and actively choose how you respond to them. When we become very dysregulated, self-regulation is often inaccessible, and therefore we need others to help us co-regulate.

Therapeutic Strokes: A stroke is a unit of recognition that you exist. It can be something physical like a handshake or a hug. It can be a verbal compliment, or non-verbal: for example, eye contact, a nod of the head or a wave of the hand. A stroke can also be a negative recognition, such as a dismissive hand gesture for a verbal 'please leave'. Positive or negative, they both acknowledge your presence and existence. Generally, strokes are considered to happen in person. We do not get the same kind of acknowledgment of our existence online. However, I would argue that things like Instagram and Facebook 'likes' could also be considered strokes in the online world.

Tolerance: This is our willingness to accept the differences between us and others in the form of feelings, behaviours and beliefs. It allows us to be social creatures. Learning the art of tolerance is a social skill we absolutely need to function in relationships. We mostly learn the skill of tolerance via the modelling we see in others and how they work with our own differences. In other words, the more tolerant people have been with you, the more tolerant you are likely to be with others.

Window of tolerance: The concept developed by Professor Dan Siegel refers to the emotional and social arousal zone that you can cope with in a healthy way. You know you are outside of your window of tolerance when your behaviour changes, and you experience either hyperarousal or hypoarousal. In a hyper state you might find yourself feeling out of control or anxious, and you may start shouting and crossing boundaries. In a hypo state, on the other hand, you might find yourself feeling numb, depressed, zoned out and exhausted.

ABOUT THE AUTHOR

<u>Zoë Aston</u> is a London-based psychotherapist, speaker, author and mum of two. She has an MSc in Psychology and Counselling. For more than a decade Zoë specialised in addiction and eating disorders, working at residential and day treatment centres in Central London. She then went on to set up her own therapy practice and released her first book titled *Your Mental Health Workout* in 2021.

She is the founder of the website www.yourmentalhealthworkout.com, and you can see more about her private practice and corporate work at www.zoeaston.com.

Zoë is herself in recovery from a long history of addiction, eating disorders, co-dependency and self-harm. She holds the belief that 'we are born into and out of relationship, therefore most of our yearning in life stems from difficulties in relationships either with others, or indeed ourselves. We learn to cover up the pain with untruths, adaptations of ourselves, perfectionism, people pleasing, denial and lying. As we get older, food, shopping, alcohol, drugs, screens can also become ways in which we channel our relational difficulties. If you've dabbled in any of these behaviours, the likelihood is the pain you are trying to treat is rooted in your relationships. In order to feel free we need to focus on the relational experience, not the symptom that treats it.'

Her second book, *Building Bonds: Why We Choose the People We Choose and How to Change it (if we want to)*, sets out to help everyone who is interested in understanding their relational choices in life so far and how to futureproof all types of relationships going forward.

Reflections

Building Bonds began life as a book idea from Studio Press's commissioning editor Ellie Rose, who pitched the concept to my lovely agent Ben, at the Soho Agency in 2022. I felt really interested in the concept as well as privileged that Bonnier Books wanted me to write it for them. After writing *Your Mental Health Workout: A 5 Week Programme to a Healthier, Happier Mind*, which offers very practical solutions for anyone who wants to work on their mental health, I was keen to share more about the human experience of relationships in a grounded and accessible way.

It would be an understatement to say that writing this book has been different to writing my first. Whilst writing *Your Mental Health Workout*, I was childless and living alone in lockdown – meaning I had all the time I needed to get things done. Writing a book felt easy! This time round I had become a wife with a baby who grew into a toddler during the course of writing this book and I became pregnant with my second child and, in fact, finished editing this book on the day he was due to be born! Squeezing chunks of writing in to any space I could find childcare for as well as nap times, early mornings and late nights, was how this came together. It had its benefits – lots of time for reflection in-between as well new relational experiences which certainly contributed to the material I've shared here.

But I have to say, if it wasn't for the help, love and flexibility of my husband, my parents, Nicole, my daughter's first childminder as well as Malakah who graciously took on the task of helping me while I was heavily pregnant and then also with my newborn while the finishing touches to the book were being arranged, I am not sure this book would have been written. I need to thank my mum specifically for questioning and gently challenging my desire to write this book in the same year I became a first-time mum – I'm not quite sure what I was thinking at the time! And also to Bonnier Books for patiently waiting for me to emerge out of the post-partum trenches and supporting me to deliver this project a year later than planned. Thank you to Frankie Jones, for being the gentle, helpful and insightful commissioning editor that you are. And also thank you to Justin Lewis for reviewing my words with such care, asking all the right questions and checking my work so thoroughly. And of course the lovely Alessandro Susin who spent so much time designing the book to complete the readers' experience.

I also always feel grateful towards my therapy clients – writing this type of book alongside them reminds me how I am as grateful to them as they are to me. My client work provides me with a wealth of experience I would not have had access to and motivates me to think differently about relationships as well as do the research that needs to be done to make sure I am helping people the best way I can. And also, thanks to my social media followers for supporting my ideas when I share them online and helping me gather an even more varied experience than I would gain in any other way.

I really hope anyone who reads this book comes away with what they needed. If you don't feel you have, please let me know, maybe your ideas will make it into the next book!

BUILDING BONDS

NOTES

BUILDING BONDS

NOTES

BUILDING BONDS